UNEQUAL BENEFITS

Privatization and Public Education in Canada

UTP insights

UTP Insights is an innovative collection of brief books offering accessible introductions to the ideas that shape our world. Each volume in the series focuses on a contemporary issue, offering a fresh perspective anchored in scholarship. Spanning a broad range of disciplines in the social sciences and humanities, the books in the UTP Insights series contribute to public discourse and debate and provide a valuable resource for instructors and students.

For a list of the books published in this series, see page 187.

UNEQUAL BENEFITS

Privatization and Public Education in Canada

Sue Winton

UNIVERSITY OF TORONTO PRESS
Toronto Buffalo London

© University of Toronto Press 2022
Toronto Buffalo London
utorontopress.com

ISBN 978-1-4875-0858-6 (cloth)   ISBN 978-1-4875-3855-2 (EPUB)
ISBN 978-1-4875-2596-5 (paper)   ISBN 978-1-4875-3854-5 (PDF)

Library and Archives Canada Cataloguing in Publication

Title: Unequal benefits : privatization and public education in Canada /
    Sue Winton.
Names: Winton, Sue, author.
Description: Includes index.
Identifiers: Canadiana (print) 20220245878 | Canadiana (ebook) 20220245908 |
    ISBN 9781487525965 (softcover) | ISBN 9781487508586 (hardcover) |
    ISBN 9781487538552 (EPUB) | ISBN 9781487538545 (PDF)
Subjects: LCSH: Privatization in education – Government policy – Canada. |
    LCSH: Education and state – Canada. | LCSH: Privatization in education –
    Canada. | LCSH: Public schools – Canada.
Classification: LCC LB2806.36 .W56 2022 | DDC 379.71 – dc23

We wish to acknowledge the land on which the University of Toronto
Press operates. This land is the traditional territory of the Wendat, the
Anishnaabeg, the Haudenosaunee, the Métis, and the Mississaugas of the
Credit First Nation.

University of Toronto Press acknowledges the financial support of the
Government of Canada, the Canada Council for the Arts, and the Ontario
Arts Council, an agency of the Government of Ontario, for its publishing
activities.

Canada Council   Conseil des Arts
for the Arts   du Canada

ONTARIO ARTS COUNCIL
CONSEIL DES ARTS DE L'ONTARIO
an Ontario government agency
un organisme du gouvernement de l'Ontario

Funded by the   Financé par le
Government   gouvernement
of Canada   du Canada

Canadä

Contents

List of Tables   vii

1 Educational Privatization and Public Education in Canada   3

2 Researching Education Privatization: Traditional and Critical
  Approaches   31

3 Funding Advantage in Public Schools   43

4 Securing Private Benefits   74

5 Taking Action   115

Appendix: Steps in Conducting Critical Policy Research   131

Notes   147

Index   175

Tables

1 Public and Quasi-Public School Types 23
2 Racial Categories across Selected In-school Programs 2011–12 (Excluding Gifted and Special Education) 86
3 Approximate Base Funding Per Student Allocated to Private Schools 101

UNEQUAL BENEFITS

Privatization and Public Education in Canada

chapter one

Educational Privatization and Public Education in Canada

As a kid there was little that could compare with the excitement I felt when a big box from Scholastic arrived in my public school classroom. I knew the time I'd spent poring over the colourful flyer debating between a new novel or an unauthorized biography of a hot musician was about to pay off. I waited with much anticipation as the teacher called out students' names and handed them their books; there was nothing worse than hearing that the one you'd ordered was out of stock. I still have a few books from those days kicking around, including a guide to writing that promised to be an invaluable resource for years to come. I passed it on to my sons.

Many years later, I was thrilled to be the one handing out the Scholastic book-order forms in my grade 5 classroom, in a school just north of the one I'd attended. I set the due date, collected students' money and completed order slips, and carefully filled out the class order form, tallying up the total number of Captain Underpants, Pokémon, *and other books requested. I calculated the grand total, wrote a cheque, and chose the "free" books for the classroom my students' orders netted me. Those books travelled with me to my next school and helped me fill a class library that never seemed full enough. When I left teaching, I passed many of them on to other teachers I knew.*

When my son started kindergarten, the thrill of the Scholastic book order returned. As though no time had passed, I found myself once again selecting books, counting coins, and sending off my order form, this time to my son's teacher. Yet his school offered something none of mine had: the Scholastic book fair. Twice a year, parent volunteers sold books, posters, and small toys ("crap," one of the parent leaders called it) to raise money that could be used to buy books for the library and other classroom materials. I happened to be volunteering in my son's classroom one day during one of the fairs, and I accompanied the teacher and children on their class visit. A note had been sent home a few days prior, telling parents that the students would be visiting the fair and inviting them to send money in with their children if they wished. And there I found myself supposedly helping the children select books. But not all the four- and five-year-olds understood that only some kids would actually be taking them home while others were "just looking." One of the children handed me a book and said, "I want this one." Knowing this child hadn't brought in any cash, I fumbled over my words, eventually telling him he'd have to go home and ask his parents for money; he wouldn't be getting the book that day. The child began to cry, and I hated what I'd said, hated the teacher and school for putting me in that position, and hated the Scholastic book fair.

I begin by sharing my experiences above for a few reasons. To begin, the narrative introduces the topic of this book, education privatization. Education privatization broadly refers to growing private sector involvement in public education, including an emphasis on its private benefits over collective ones. The story illustrates the presence, appeal, and some of the problems associated with private sector involvement in public schools. In it we see how private money flows into schools in ways that benefit parents' own children,[1] potentially other people's children, their kids' classrooms and schools, and, of course, Scholastic, a business. The account shows also, I hope, that I understand why parents and educators participate in fundraising initiatives such as book sales. It also highlights the reality, however, that not all kids and parents choose to or are able to take part. It raises questions about who should pay for classroom resources and school libraries, whether kids should spend class time shopping, if parents who act as salespeople for Scholastic should be compensated, and how we feel about some children in Canada's public schools having access to books and resources that other children do not. My story also demonstrates that fundraising in public schools is not new, although schools' reliance on it is greater than ever in many places.

This book focuses on a range of policies facilitating education privatization across the country, and I've written it with different audiences in mind. For parents of school-age children like me, I hope the book helps you see how policies that invite us to make choices that benefit our own children may simultaneously disadvantage other kids and our democracy. Please know this book is not meant as an indictment of any group of parents. Indeed, I suspect few caregivers, if any, set out to privatize public education, but I aim to show that their decisions may nevertheless have that effect. The same may true for another imagined group of readers: policymakers. By reviewing research from Canada and beyond, I show that many policies introduced at the school, district, and provincial levels in the last few decades call upon and enable private actors to take on responsibilities that prioritize individual benefits over collective ones. I argue that these policies must be changed so that our public schools can realize their democratic potential. This book is also written for members of the general public interested in understanding how certain education policies contribute to social inequalities. I hope to convince all these readers that we need to resist growing privatization in Canadian public education and suggest some ways that we might go about doing this work.

This book is also for education policy researchers interested in educational privatization. I hope to bring research knowledge about Canada's experiences into international conversations about the phenomenon. Much of this literature exposes the same harmful impacts that school choice, fundraising, and other policies privatizing public education have on disadvantaged groups found elsewhere, and it challenges popular perceptions of Canadian schools – and Canada itself – as sites of diversity, opportunity, and equity.

For students of education policy (whether enrolled in a formal program or not), this book provides an introduction to critical policy research by explaining what distinguishes it from traditional approaches and highlights how policies are inherently political. If you are interested in learning how to conduct a formal critical policy study you will want to check out the appendix. The book, however, invites all readers to adopt a critical stance towards policy by asking *"Who are the policy's winners and who are its losers?"* and *"What role does this policy play in supporting or challenging the status quo?"*

What's New about Education Privatization in Canada?

In Canada, a federal state, the country's ten provincial and three territorial governments are each responsible for the education of their residents. Despite the absence of a federal department of education or national curriculum, the provinces and territories nevertheless have similar education systems.[2] Structurally, they all have a ministry of education led by a minister of education (an elected member of the government) and school boards consisting of democratically elected trustees who set policies and procedures for local schools. They have similar approaches to financing schools and to teacher education, and most have outcomes-based curricula and large-scale student assessments.[3] They also have relatively well-supported public education.

For one thing, the vast majority of kids – 92 per cent – attend public schools across the country. Even in British Columbia (BC), the province with the lowest attendance rate, more than 86 per cent go to a public school. This proportion is more than 98 per cent in New Brunswick, Nunavut, the Northwest Territories, and Newfoundland and Labrador.[4] Research provides additional evidence of support. A 2005 survey of parents across Canada found that 72 per cent of parents gave their local public schools an A or B grade; only 8 per cent rated them D or F.[5] In Ontario, where more than 94 per cent of kids go to public school, a 2018 survey of attitudes towards public education found that 50 per cent of the public (including parents) and 61 per cent of parents with kids in schools are either Very Satisfied or Somewhat Satisfied with the school system.[6] Satisfaction is higher in Alberta. A 2019 survey found 90 per cent of parents and 69 per cent of Albertans are satisfied with the quality of education in the province.[7] And 83 per cent of parents with kids in BC's K–12 schools reported that their child's experience has been either Very Positive or Moderately Positive.[8]

High levels of support for public schooling in Canada are not new. Michael Mindzak, an assistant professor at Brock University, explains that "Canadians have long valued public schools for their sense of community and promotion of national identity and citizenship, and they have seemingly remained committed to many of these ideals into the twenty-first century."[9] Canadian students' consistently strong performance on international tests, such as the Organisation for Economic Co-operation and Development's Programme for International Student Assessment, may also help explain why the public remains confident in the country's public schools despite concerted efforts by some governments and reform advocates to convince Canadians that their confidence is misplaced.

Nevertheless, I'm worried about the privatization of public education in Canada. One of my concerns relates to a key reason I think support for public education remains high: *because* public systems have become more private-like. That is, over the past few decades governments and school districts have adopted policies that encourage private actors to take on roles and responsibilities formerly provided by the public sector. They have also given parents more choice and voice in their children's schools – influence and options that some parents desire.[10] I focus on a number of these policies in this book, including school fundraising, fees, international education, and school choice policies. All of them enable some kids to benefit more from public schools than others. I hope the research I share prompts readers to reflect on the consequences of education policy choices pursued across the country in the past twenty-five years or so and motivates them to fight for more just – and more public – education systems.

There is also evidence that support for public education is declining. The 2018 Ontario survey I mentioned above shows that levels of public and parental satisfaction and confidence in the province's public schools are lower than they were in 2012, when they were at the highest levels. At the same time, while most kids attend public schools, the number of kids going to private schools and being homeschooled is slowly increasing. According to Statistics Canada, the number of kids enrolled in private schools rose 2 per cent across Canada in the year between 2015–16 and 2016–17. In the five years between 2012–13 and 2016–17 the overall proportion of kids in private school increased from 6.8 per cent to 7.2 per cent while enrolment in public schools decreased 0.6 per cent in the same period. In 2016–17, a little more than 7 per cent of Canadian students attended a private school, though there is considerable variation across the provinces.[11] At 13 per cent, BC had the highest proportion of kids enrolled in private schools. Next was Quebec with 9.5 per cent. Newfoundland and Labrador, PEI, and New Brunswick have the lowest numbers at 1.5 per cent, 1.4 per cent and 1.1 per cent respectively. Finally, the number of kids homeschooled between 2007 and 2012 increased 23 per cent across the country.[12]

Researchers Lynn Bosetti, Deani Van Pelt, and Derek Allison offer a number of reasons families choose private schools in Canada.[13] Many parents want their children to receive religious instruction; indeed, almost half of the country's private schools are faith-based. Other parents are looking for specialized programs that will address their kids' special interests or needs. Some seek alternative pedagogical approaches, such as those offered by Montessori or Waldorf schools, or resources and extracurricular options not found as readily in public schools. Some parents choose private schools to escape from public education because they believe government curricula is too politically correct, the school environment is unsafe, or that teachers are complacent. Some families hope to expand their kids' social networks, while others find the increasing online instruction options available through private schools attractive. Not to be overlooked, of course, is the reality that private school parents, as paying customers, may be able to have their demands met in ways that aren't possible or tolerated in public schools. They may want – and indeed get – more say in their children's education.

When it comes to homeschooling, before the COVID-19 pandemic many parents choosing this option did so as a way to design their kids' education around their unique needs and talents, to pass on their family's values, to provide a safer learning environment, or to practically accommodate a busy lifestyle.[14]

Education Privatization: Variations and a Definition

Growing numbers of kids attending private schools or being homeschooled are only two examples of education privatization. There are many more. In an article that situates education privatization within the broader trend of public sector privatization, US researcher Chris Lubienski outlines a typology of privatization that captures some of its variants:

1 The transfer of ownership from the public to the private sector (e.g., sale of Air Canada)
2 The provision of services by a private company paid for by the public (e.g., city governments paying a private company to collect garbage)
3 Increased private control over public resources (e.g., public-private partnerships)
4 Greater private responsibility for paying for resources and services previously funded by governments (e.g., students paying higher percentage of university costs through tuition)
5 Provision or production of public services modelled on practices of the private sector (e.g., running a hospital like a business)
6 Change in emphasis of the provision or production of a good from a collective orientation to an individual focus[15]

What these variations of privatization all have in common is the movement of one or more aspects of a public good or service (i.e., its ownership, provision, governance, funding, orientation) to the private sector. Privatization does not require the wholesale transfer of all these aspects of a public good to the private sector in order to be said to have taken place. Early research on education privatization emphasized this point by defining the phenomenon as "a *process* or a *trajectory* whereby the public-sector is gradually displaced by private-sector activity."[16]

Researchers Stephen Ball and Deborah Youdell, like Lubienski, recognize the complexity of education privatization and described two types: exogenous privatization and endogenous privatization.[17] *Exogenous privatization* involves bringing the private sector into public schools to take on roles once fulfilled by the public sector. These include funding schools, building and managing infrastructure, teaching, creating curriculum, training teachers, and making education policy. It's important to note that the private sector includes civil-society actors, such as religious institutions, non-government organizations, philanthropists, foundations, as well as parents and other caregivers, not only businesses. Governments play a key role in transforming education by introducing policies that facilitate exogenous privatization. Enabling policies include those that encourage or permit fundraising in public schools, contracting out work to private companies, hiring private consultants, sharing costs through public-private partnerships (sometimes referred to as PPPs or P3s), selling educational services and materials, establishing private schools that offer single-credit courses, marketing and selling products in schools, recruiting tuition-paying students from outside Canada, and many more. Not all of these policies have been introduced recently nor for the express purpose of privatizing education, however. Some aspects of the private sector, such as textbook publishing, have long histories of involvement with public education systems.

Endogenous privatization, or what Heather-jane Robertson refers to as "privatization by stealth,"[18] involves introducing ideas, practices, and values of the for-profit sector into public education – essentially "moving the private sector into public schools."[19] Two key complementary strategies facilitate this shift in education: the creation of educational markets and New Public Management (NPM).[20] To understand what it means to organize an education system as a market, imagine a store where customers choose between products based on various kinds of information (e.g., quality, uniqueness, price) as well as their own preferences, needs, and resources. Sellers compete by creating desired and unique products of varying quality and marketing them to consumers. In marketized education systems, the products are specialized schools and programs, the consumers are parents and their children, and information provided to inform choices includes graduation rates, standardized test scores, and school rankings. Policies that create and promote school markets include Alberta's *Charter Schools Regulation* that permits "autonomous, non-profit public schools designed to provide innovative or enhanced education programs" and open enrolment policies that allow children to attend any school in their districts (Quebec) or province (BC). Specialized programs offered in addition to the regular school program by many districts across the country, such as French Immersion and the International Baccalaureate, are also part of education marketplaces.

I closely examine policies that encourage marketization in Canadian public education in chapter 4.

The second major strategy of education privatization, NPM, involves a new form of governing the public sector. NPM involves a wide array of practices modelled on those in the private sector including an emphasis on standards, performance measures, accountability, and results.[21] In education, NPM policies and practices include standardized curricula, large-scale assessments, graduation-rate targets, and public school rankings. The role of school principals in an NPM model shifts from a school's educational leader to the manager of compliance with government policies and its success, including its ability to recruit students and its students' performance on standardized tests.[22] Indeed, NPM changes the culture of public schools as principals, teachers, and parents are assigned new roles and responsibilities. Research shows that teachers, for example, lose some of their autonomy when they have to teach a more tightly prescribed curriculum that aligns with standardized tests written by their students.[23]

Endogenous and exogenous forms of privatization often work together. Many specialized programs, for example, charge parents fees to cover additional program costs. A specialized athletic program offered by the York Region District School Board in Ontario, for example, charges $30 to apply, $350 for a uniform package, a $100 program fee, a $35 activity fee, and $30 for grade 9 orientation.[24] The idea that governments are responsible for providing only what is necessary and that people who want more than the basics should pay for it is borrowed from the private sector, where fee structures are commonplace.[25]

Various forms of endogenous and exogenous education privatization give rise to the sixth kind of privatization identified in Lubienski's typology: the emphasis of public education shifts towards prioritizing individual benefits over collective ones. That is, people begin to see public education as primarily about accruing individual benefits rather than mainly for the greater good of society. In chapters 3 and 4 I examine how some parents use their resources in efforts to secure benefits and advantages for their own children in public schools that are not available to everyone. Fundraising, paying for private psychological assessments to access special education services, and private tutoring are three such examples.

Paths to Education Privatization

Importantly, privatization is not a phenomenon that just *happens* to schools, much like rain falls on their roofs. Referring to this process as a noun disguises the reality that people are *actively privatizing* public education through their policies and practices, even if they don't recognize it. It is policymakers who introduce policies that promote school choice and permit school fees, and it's school district leaders who recruit tuition-paying international students to offset budget shortfalls (determined, of course, by elected officials). It's parents who choose between school programs, and it's shareholders of companies such as SchoolCash Online and Scholastic that make money from public school initiatives. While I use the term education privatization throughout this book, both because it is simple and because it is how researchers typically refer to various actors' diverse privatizing practices, it's important to remember that it is *people* who privatize, and it's people who can choose to do otherwise.

So how do people privatize public education? In 2016 Antoni Verger, Clara Fontdevila, and Adrián Zancajo published *The Privatization of Education: A Political Economy of Global Education Reform*. In it the authors present findings from their investigation of why countries around the world adopt privatization policies and how nations' historical, economic, and political contexts impact what they look like in practice. Using a systematic literature review methodology, they analysed 227 studies of privatization in elementary and secondary education published between 1999 and 2014 in English, Portuguese, Spanish, and French to determine patterns of this phenomenon across the globe. They identified six paths to privatization:

1 **Education privatization as a state reform**: the ideological road to privatization in Chile and the United Kingdom.
2 **Education privatization in social democratic welfare states**: the Nordic path towards privatization.

3 **Scaling up privatization**: school choice reforms in the United States.
4 **Privatization by default in low income countries**: the emergence and expansion of low-fee private schools.
5 **Historical public-private partnerships**: the cases of the Netherlands, Belgium, and Spain.
6 **Along the path of emergency**: privatization by way of catastrophe.[26]

Verger and his co-authors conclude that Canada, like the United States, has followed the path of scaling up privatization. In countries that have followed this path, they explain, "the adoption of pro-private sector reforms, predominantly at the subnational level, have eventually resulted in the alteration of the governance of the public education system."[27]

To illustrate how this path unfolds, the authors focus largely on the charter schools movement in the United States. While I agree with Verger and his colleagues' characterization of Canada's path towards privatization, given that Alberta is currently the only province with charter schools, I don't think their example is appropriate or helpful for people hoping to understand what is taking place in Canadian school systems. In this book I use policies common across the country to show that Canada is indeed on a "scaling up path toward privatization."[28]

In fairness to Verger and his co-authors, they explain that they focus on the United States case in part because of the large volume of studies that examine it, and they refer readers to Adam Davidson-Harden and Suzanne Majhanovich's research on education privatization in Canada. Davidson-Harden and Majhanovich's study, published in 2004, highlighted a number of trends indicating that public education was privatizing.[29] One of the trends they discussed was increased private funding of public schools. They noted this was occurring through higher levels of parent and community fundraising for schools, recruitment of tuition-paying international students by school boards, and teachers' practice of paying for teaching materials with their own money. Davidson-Harden and Majhanovich suggested that interest in PPPs, arrangements in which private entities provide funds to build infrastructure used by public organizations, was high and that there was a possibility of PPPs in the future. They reported growing enrolment in private schools and new means of funding private education with public dollars as additional indicators of increasing education privatization in some provinces. They also pointed to the introduction and promotion of charter schools in Alberta while regular public schools remained underfunded.

One of my objectives in writing this book is to provide an update on a number of the trends identified by Davidson-Harden and Majhanovich. I show in chapter 3, for example, that private funding of public education through school fees and fundraising has intensified; in chapter 4, I highlight that public funding for various forms of private schooling has also increased and discuss initiatives introduced since 2004 to encourage parents to opt for private schooling, such as the Children First: School Choice Trust grants. I also examine some forms of privatization that Davidson-Harden and Majhanovich did not address, most notably the expansion and inequitable outcomes of quasi-markets within public school systems as well as strategies parents use outside school buildings to provide their kids with individual advantages *inside* public schools. Ultimately, I demonstrate that education privatization continues to grow and diversify across Canada.

However, I don't address every facet of education privatization in the country. For one thing, I limit my focus to elementary and secondary education only. There is a lot of research that demonstrates that Canada's higher education systems are privatizing as well.[30] And while I acknowledge the long history of corporate involvement in public schools and see it as an important historical influence on contemporary privatization trends, I don't focus on it. My discussion of practices borrowed from the private sector is also limited to a handful. There are simply more variants of education privatization than I can cover. However, in the book's final chapter I suggest further reading and resources where you can learn more about other manifestations of education privatization.

I focus on policies that enable – if not outright encourage – parents to act in ways that provide advantages to their own children not available to all kids in publicly funded schools. Again, I know that parents make choices about their children's education for reasons that have nothing to do with a desire to privatize public schools, but that doesn't mean their decisions don't have that impact. And parents don't act alone, of course; many well-meaning educators and policymakers champion policies that reproduce inequities. My experiences as a researcher, university professor, teacher educator, and parent have shown me that many people don't understand how their individual choices contribute to broader patterns of social inequality. Making these connections visible is another of the book's key objectives. Knowledge of one's participation in reproducing this unequal system can be difficult, but understanding how policies make us complicit is important in the pursuit of more equitable schools. This knowledge enables us to resist our policy-specified roles in education privatization and advocate for robust systems of public education.

Contexts of Education Privatization in Canada

Education privatization, particularly *exogenous* privatization, is not new in Canadian public schools. In her book, *Captive Audience: How Corporations Invaded Our Schools*, Catherine Gidney traces the history of corporate involvement in public education in Canada since the early 1900s.[31] She explains that in the first half of the twentieth century, businesses created and sponsored materials for teachers to use in their classrooms, such as books, posters, maps, and teachers' guides. Companies also paid for school trips, provided free teacher training, hosted contests, and ran after-school programs for kids. They also sponsored films for classroom use. Some banks and credit unions opened branches in schools. Many educators welcomed the materials and opportunities offered by businesses because schools were often short on money and up-to-date textbooks. They also provided teachers with access to new information, and some believed the resources were useful teaching tools. Corporations recognized schools as important sites for advertising to children since kids were increasingly involved (and influential) in their parents' purchasing decisions and were emerging as a distinct segment of consumers.

While various sponsorships and donations continued throughout the twentieth century, Gidney demonstrates that corporations'
involvement took on new forms in the 1980s and 1990s. For example, as new high school courses in marketing and consumer education were introduced, companies developed curriculum materials
for classroom use and offered tours of their facilities. They also do-
nated equipment and outdated computers. Banks offered financial
literacy programs, while some businesses introduced literacy initiatives (e.g., Pizza Hut, McDonald's, Northern Telecom, Toronto
Dominion Bank Financial).

The business community also showed a growing interest in
education policy as it wanted to see more emphasis on preparing
students for the workforce. Formal partnerships between governments, school boards, and the private sector that would offer
supposedly long-term, mutual benefits to all parties (as opposed
to one-time donations to individual schools or districts) became
commonplace. Sometimes students worked in businesses where
they earned credits and received training. The partnerships also
introduced students to possible careers in the private sector. The
partnerships offered businesses a positive public image and enabled some to access school facilities, instructional opportunities for
employees, and student feedback on new products.

Technology companies were particularly interested in creating
partnerships. Schools were a huge market for computer hardware
and software sales, and technology companies, including Apple
and Commodore Business Machines, offered them generous dis-
counts. Technology corporations also recognized students as also
future customers. Educators, parents, and policymakers widely
supported technology companies' involvement in schools, believing computers and other technology engaged students, promoted
learning, and prepared students for jobs of the twenty-first century.
Critics' concerns about unproven claims of technology's educational benefits were marginalized. So, too, were their worries about
the increased emphasis of public schooling on workforce preparation and diminished attention to other purposes of education.

Changes in the ways corporations engaged with schools and
education policy reflected the rise of neoliberal ideas and beliefs

about how the world should be organized.[32] Propelled by the economic crisis of the 1970s, neoliberal ideology began its ascent in Canada in the 1980s; today neoliberal ideas are dominant here and in much of the world.[33] A central neoliberal idea is that the economic and social world should be organized according to the principles of the free market. That is, individuals, organizations, and businesses should be able to compete for success with minimal government involvement. Above I encouraged you to think about how supermarkets compete for customers in open markets. You could also consider the airline industry. Airlines compete for passengers by offering them various benefits (e.g., lower ticket prices, unique flight routes, special onboard entertainment), and in turn, potential customers weigh different airlines' offerings and choose the one that best suits their interests. The need to attract customers supposedly forces airlines to continually strive to improve their services and respond to passengers' demands. At the same time, airlines are trying to make money. To increase profitability, they must be efficient (i.e., cost effective) and so they might cut costs associated with flying (e.g., reduce the number of employees, decrease weight of airplanes). A now-familiar practice in the race for market share in many industries is businesses' use of short-term job contracts rather than permanent positions so they can quickly respond to changing market conditions (i.e., they can easily get rid of staff to manage costs).

Rather than disappearing all together, in a market-oriented society an important role of governments is to create new markets and facilitate conditions that enable markets to thrive.[34] They normally accomplish this work through introducing new policies. They've done this in the private sector in part by removing or loosening controls over banking, currency exchanges, capital movement, corporate taxes, and trade.[35] They have also cut public spending and introduced other austerity measures to encourage economic growth.[36] These efforts have created markets that operate on a global scale, and governments today focus on ensuring that their states can compete successfully in the global economy.

Governments have also introduced policies to encourage the public sector to be more private-like, such as the creation of education markets and introduction of NPM as described above. Policies encouraging marketization are based in part on the belief that the private sector is more efficient than the public sector because of businesses' need to compete for success. Conversely, the public sector is derided for encouraging laziness, complacency, and waste because its workers don't have to worry about going out of operation. NPM is a strategy to reform and improve the quality of public services within a context of reduced public funding.[37]

Within education markets new actors take on roles that were formerly taken on by governments. In public education systems, principals become marketers as they try to attract students, for example, and as I discuss in later chapters, parents are asked to be funders, governors, producers, and consumers.[38]

The call for parents to take on these roles reflects the broader neoliberal objectives to dismantle society and a social state in favour of "free, responsibilized individuals."[39] Political theorist Wendy Brown explains in her book, *In the Ruins of Neoliberalism*, that neoliberals reject the idea of society existing separate from individuals, and thus they reject the idea that governments should pursue a predetermined plan, including plans oriented towards social justice.[40] Rather, individuals should be free to pursue their interests by following naturally arising (i.e., not government imposed) rules of moral and market conduct.[41] It is their responsibility, not a government's, to meet their needs (and those of their families) and ensure their success.[42] An individual's failure is thus understood as a consequence of their poor choices rather than inequitable policies, structural inequalities, racism, sexism, or other societal factors. This perspective fits nicely with Canadians' belief in meritocracy: that is, the idea that people who work hard deserve their success.

Education policies that ask parents to choose and fund their kids' school programs reflect these neoliberal ideas; they place responsibility for ensuring that their children receive a suitable education on parents rather than the government. Understandably, most parents will do whatever they can to help their children be successful in a competitive market. There is a considerable body of research that shows middle class parents are particularly anxious about this role. And as I will show in later chapters, many embrace, if not outright demand, privatization of public education as a means of securing advantages for their children.

Neoliberal ideas are not the only ideas that propel education privatization. Also important are those that fall under the umbrella of neoconservatism. Canadian scholar Ann Porter explains that neoconservatism is a set of ideas that advocates traditional family structures, values, and discipline.[43] It looks to governments to play a strong role in maintaining social and moral order by supporting religion, traditional family values, and the law. While they differ in their expectations of government, both neoconservatism and neoliberalism reflect a fear of losing control. The fear may be the loss of personal or economic security, traditional values or knowledge, and/or predictable social roles and relations.[44] Education theorist Michael Apple explains that this fear creates an "us" versus "them" distinction wherein "they" – the poor and immigrants who are "lazy, immoral, and permissive" – are a threat to "us" – members of dominant groups who are "law-abiding, hardworking, decent and virtuous."[45] Such ideas were promoted through policy and practices by Ontario's PC government in the 1990s,[46] and they are evident in contemporary character education, entrepreneurial education, and discipline policies in Canada.[47] Neoconservatism combined with the ideas of meritocracy and responsibilized individualism reinforces the belief that some people are more deserving than others of social benefits, including public education.

Neoliberal and neoconservative ideas circulate globally to inform contemporary education policies, including education privatization. The exchange of policy ideas happens in many ways: through conferences and international organizations (such as the World Bank and the Organization for Economic Cooperation and Development); when international students return to their home countries; and via policy entrepreneurs who advocate favoured policy solutions.[48] In particular, education policy is increasingly developed by policy networks that often include non-traditional actors in education: businesses, government officials, think tanks, and philanthropists and their foundations. Individuals often hold multiple positions in the organizations that make up these networks, and their positions overlap and shift. Policy networks operate within and across individual countries and education jurisdictions.

As suggested by the six paths to privatization identified by Verger and his colleagues, the trend towards privatization is not unique to Canada. In Chile, for example, the federal government introduced competition between private and public schools by creating vouchers that parents could use to pay private school tuition.[49] In Uganda, the government partnered with private schools to deliver secondary education,[50] while for-profit teacher-education providers and private tutoring centres have been established in Ireland.[51] In Australia, the Government of Victoria contracted out public school cleaning to private companies.[52] These are only a handful of cases of education privatization across the world. The phenomenon is truly global.

Public Education and the Public School Ideal

Education privatization is not without its critics. Critical policy researchers, public education advocates, teacher unions, and many others have argued for decades that the process undermines public education. But what *defines* public education and why is it worth protecting? Based on research in Alberta and Northern England, Australian researchers Nicole Mockler, Anna Hogan, Bob Lingard, Mark Rahimi, and Greg Thompson identified at least four meanings of "public" in people's references to contemporary public education.[53] In some cases they mean public *control* of schools (ownership, hiring authority, regulation, legal basics, tax status). They might also mean public *access* (enrolment, resources, curriculum, competitive, school choice) or *funding* (public expenditure, parent contributions, enrolments, profit, philanthropy). Finally, some refer to aspects of school *teaching* (staffing, professional development, accreditations orientation to teaching, unionization).

Scholars Jon Young, Ben Levin, and Dawn Wallin outlined defining characteristics of public education in Canada.[54] Some are the same as those identified by Mockler and her colleagues. First is the idea of *universal access*: everyone of school age should be able to attend school for free. Second, costs associated with schooling are *paid for by government* so the ability to pay does not impact the quality of schooling a child receives. Third, all students have *equal opportunity* to reap the benefits of schooling. The fact that *decisions are made through public political processes* is a fourth element. Finally, schools must serve the *public's interest*; that is, they are accountable to the public for the quality and content of schooling. In this book, I will refer to a school that contains all these features as one that reflects the *public school ideal*.

Looking across Canada, few so-called public schools reflect this ideal. The child attending the elementary school on her block in Charlottetown, the middle schooler studying at a charter school in Edmonton, and a teen completing online courses in a BC private school can all be said to be attending public schools – depending on whether you view public access, control, funding, or accountability as a defining feature. Given that provinces and territories in Canada are responsible for education and the differing histories of each one, variation between them is not unexpected. In Ontario, for example, whether a school is considered public or not typically depends on whether it receives its funding from the government rather than through tuition. However, as I discuss in chapter 3, most public schools in the province actually generate funds from private sources as well. In BC, private schools (or "independent schools" as they prefer to be called) receive some government funding. University of British Columbia researchers Wendy Poole and Gerald Fallon describe them as *"quasi-public"* (emphasis in original) since they are partially funded by the public.[55] In fact, the term *quasi-public* can be applied to other variations of the public school ideal as well; these schools contain some combination of universal access, government funding, equal opportunity, public decision-making, and privileging public interest, but not all of them. I discuss each of these characteristics of the public school ideal later as I consider how and in what ways school systems across the country reflect each one.

To begin, all provinces and territories *do* provide access to free schooling for all their resident children. However, not all kids have access to the same kinds of public schools within and across

Canada. Newfoundland and Labrador, for example, has just two publicly funded systems (English or French secular), while Ontario has four (French Catholic; English Catholic; French secular, and English secular). An Ontario child's right to attend schools in one or more of these systems depends on whether their parents are French speaking and if they are Catholic (until the end of elementary school). Table 1 outlines various configurations of public and quasi-public schools across Canada. Notably, most schools in "publicly-funded education systems" generate funds from sources other than governments.

As I discuss in chapter 4, there is an increasing variety of specialized programs and schools available *within* public education systems, such as French Immersion and specialized arts, athletics, science, and technology programs. However, universal access to these programs is not guaranteed, and the programs may charge fees to cover their costs. Restricted admittance to specialized programs and their associated fees are two ways they violate the public school ideal, and their growing number exemplifies education privatization. In fact, all provincial and territorial governments permit schools to charge fees for materials and programs offered in addition to the basic education program paid for by governments – and many do. They charge for field trips, sports, student groups, locks, and more. In chapter 3, I discuss how school fees and other means of fundraising compromise the public school ideal by failing to ensure all kids have equal opportunity to benefit from public schooling.

Every province and territory has laws and regulations that govern schools funded by the public. As mentioned earlier and shown in Table 1, private schools in BC – as well as in Alberta, Saskatchewan, Manitoba, and Quebec – may receive public funds as well. Canadian schools that receive 100 per cent of their funding from public sources (not including voluntary fees and fundraising) are typically part of districts governed by democratically elected school boards that make decisions about the operations in their systems. Their debates are conducted *in public* and include opportunities for community members to contribute their perspectives through participating in consultations, presenting

Table 1. Public and Quasi-Public School Types

School Types	BC	AB	SK	MB	ON	QC	NB	NS	PEI	NL	YK	NW	NT
English-language schools part of publicly funded education system	X	X	X	X	X	X	X	X	X	X	X	X	X
French-language schools part of publicly funded education system	X	X	X	X	X	X	X	X	X	X	X	X	X
Catholic schools part of publicly funded education system(s)		X	X		X						X	X	
Private schools receive some government funds	X	X	X	X		X							
Charter schools receive government funds		X											
Homeschoolers receive some government funds		X	X*								X	X	X

* Varies by school district.

to the board, serving on committees, and casting votes at election time. Alberta's charter schools, the only ones in Canada, occupy a unique space. They receive the same amount of funds as regular public schools but have more autonomy in their programs and governance. Alberta's Charter School Regulations require, among other things, that charter schools hold their governing board meetings in public. However, private schools that receive partial funding are not beholden to the same levels of public control or accountability, although they must meet some criteria set by the government to qualify for funds. In chapter 4 I examine the issue of public funding of private schools in detail. I show that funding to private schools has increased over time and encourages students to attend private schools: both indicators of education privatization.

Central to the idea of public education is that its schools serve the public interest. While what constitutes the public interest is debated, it means, in part, that public schooling must prioritize public benefits over personal ones. Personal benefits of schooling include the development of one's individual potential, self-esteem, and spirituality, as well as the acquisition of skills and knowledge that can be used to secure employment and social mobility. Public benefits, on the other hand, include preparing youth for the roles and responsibilities of democratic citizenship; providing them opportunities to learn how to live peacefully with people different from themselves; fostering their concern for the environment; creating a workforce that can pay taxes and meet the needs of the economy; keeping public health care costs in check; and producing people to transform the world.[56] Schools also provide an important custodial function, as evidenced by the challenges faced by parents while kids were out of school during the COVID-19 pandemic. Politicians, parents, and employers were forced to acknowledge that the economy could not restart until children could safely attend public schools.

Critics of education privatization and other neoliberal-influenced policies in education argue that they privilege economic purposes of education over social and political purposes. In particular, they emphasize the production of skilled and flexible workers (i.e., human capital) who can ensure the competitiveness of national economies in global markets.[57] Schools are viewed primarily as sites of job preparation wherein children acquire skills, knowledge, and credentials to give themselves individual advantages in a competitive job market. As the number of well-paying and secure jobs decreases, the need for them to do so increases. As parents are expected to do whatever they can to help ensure their children's success, their choices – encouraged by education privatization – may negatively impact other people's kids.

Opponents of education privatization call on policymakers and educational leaders to reject policies that exclude some children's access to educational opportunities, rely on fundraising and other sources of private funding, limit public accountability, emphasize individual rather than collective interests, prioritize economic purposes of education, and prevent some kids from reaping the benefits of public education. Instead, they demand a recommitment to public education. Their calls might suggest a return to "better days" when public schools were fully state funded, overseen by benevolent governments, accessible to all, and vigorously in pursuit of the public good. It's important, however, not to romanticize about a version of public education that has yet to be realized.[58]

Establishment of Public Education in Canada

Advocates of Canadian public education have always been a diverse group. Those who supported the idea of mass public schooling in Canada did so for political, social, religious, and economic reasons.[59] Historian Paul Axelrod explains that one group, the colonial politicians, believed schools could provide political stability as Canada experienced major social changes, including rapid population growth, industrial development, increased commercialism in towns, and a rise in the number of people experiencing poverty. They saw schools as places where young people could learn the roles and responsibilities of citizenship while also developing emotional and cultural connections to Britain. Schools would teach students to defer to authority and to exhibit respect for property. These lessons, they hoped, would bring about the social order that Canada's economic growth required. They wanted to discourage rebellions such as those they witnessed in Upper and Lower Canada and in the United States. Indeed, some wanted Canadians to be distinctly different from their southern neighbours, who they viewed as too materialistic, aggressive, disorderly, individualistic, and fond of dissent.

Some advocates of public schooling argued that public schools could reduce the religious tensions experienced in many communities. While the schools would be technically secular, they could promote Christian values to students. Not only would this ensure all children received this type of moral education, it would also relieve religious institutions of the cost of providing education to children in their congregations.

Support for mass schooling could also be found from farmers who saw schools as providing opportunities other than farming for their children's futures. For those who would go on to farm, they would learn skills such as accounting and mechanization that would be useful to their work. The expansion of schooling would mean that their kids could attend local schools, live at home, and continue to help out on the farm. Tenant farmers in PEI in particular, Axelrod explains, believed that if their children were literate they would be better able to negotiate with landlords in their own interests.

Some promoters, dubbed "prominent 'rebels'" by Axelrod, viewed fully funded public education as an instrument of democratization.[60] They argued that education should not be for only the wealthy since "an educated populace would be better able to act in its own political interest."[61] Social reformers, on the other hand, promoted the education of poor children not for the children's sake but rather as a means to promote class harmony and safe communities. Not only could schools teach poor children middle-class norms of discipline, manners, respect, and morality, they could also promote acceptance of class differences. Middle-class citizens stood to benefit from public school expansion in another way as well: public funds for schools could be extended to cover the costs of tuition at the grammar schools attended primarily by middle-class children. Finally, emerging ideas about the nature of childhood that saw children as naturally unruly, malleable, and unreasonable generated support for mass schooling. Along with their potential for political, class, and moral socialization, some advocates saw schools as places where children could learn appropriate gender roles and to tame their sexuality.

This brief overview of the origins of public education in Canada shows public schools were founded upon a wide array of political, social, and economic goals that were supposed to serve the public as well as individual children and their families. Since their beginnings Canada's public schools have benefitted some groups much more than others: they have provided far more advantages to white, English- and French-speaking, able-bodied, and middle- and upper-class children and parents than they have to poor, disabled, Indigenous, Black, and other racialized families. Our public schools can and must change to serve all children well, but they remain our best hope for democracy.

Critical Democracy and the Public School Ideal

Public education in Canada needs to be more equitable than it was before the turn to education privatization. Indeed, achieving the public school ideal requires more than rejecting education privatization but it involves this move as well. As I show in this book, policies in our public schools that facilitate education privatization perpetuate and exacerbate inequalities that have long existed inside and outside the country's public schools.

If we want Canada to be a strong, vibrant democracy, we need schools that reflect the public school ideal. And when I refer to democracy I don't just mean a system of government. I'm advocating for a version of democracy where people live together in ways that reflect commitments to equity, inclusion, social justice, diversity, public participation in decision-making, and the public good. Canadian scholars John Portelli and Patrick Solomon refer to this version of democracy as *critical* democracy.[62] Critical democracy differs in some ways from liberal notions of democracy that emphasize representative government and privilege individual and civil rights; it also different from the idea of market democracy that emphasizes choice and consumption. As Canadian scholar Laura Pinto explains, critical democracy is centrally concerned with eliminating inequities and oppression.[63] It is committed to the pursuit of economic, social, and political justice for all.

A fair society benefits its members in myriad ways. Not only is everyone able to fully participate as peers in social life,[64] but equal societies are healthier and more socially cohesive.[65] Its members trust each other more and are more likely to help each other than in less equal places.[66]

If we hope to achieve such a society, we need schools that teach children about equality and equity and to value and respect diverse beliefs, perspectives, and ways of living. These lessons are learned not only through what educators teach explicitly but also through students' observances and daily practices.

Pursuing critical democracy demands changing education privatization policies and practices that produce inequitable access to opportunities and benefits of public education. Public schools must be fully funded by the public and accessible to the communities they serve. Wealthier people shouldn't be able to use their money to buy access or advantages for their kids, nor should funds for public schools be generated from private businesses or foundations. And public money invested in education should remain in the public domain. It should not go to private schools or businesses except when governments don't have the capacity to produce supplies such as desks and textbooks. In terms of control, decisions about education must remain with elected officials. Debates must occur in the open, and constituents must have authentic opportunities to share their ideas and perspectives. In short, if we want to achieve a socially just Canada we need to stop education privatization and pursue the public school ideal.

Chapter Overviews

In this first chapter I introduced the phenomenon of education privatization. I pointed to indications of widespread support for public education in Canada and suggested it might, ironically, be attributable in part to policies that make public schools more private-like. I described aspects of the broader policy context that support and enable education privatization, including neoliberalism, neoconservatism, and long-standing corporate involvement in Canadian public schools. Importantly, I introduced the *public school ideal*, a school that is free and accessible, provides all kids with opportunities to benefit from its offerings, prioritizes public benefits, and is accountable to the public. I argued that a strong democratic society, one that is centrally concerned with eliminating inequities and oppression, demands that we move away from education privatization and commit to pursuing the public school ideal.

In chapter 2, I provide a brief overview of the broad field of educational policy studies by introducing two general approaches to conceptualizing and studying policy: the traditional/rational approach and the critical approach. Using studies of large-scale standardized testing in Canada as illustrative examples,

I highlight how the two approaches differ in terms of their beliefs about the nature of the social world and the purposes of policy research. I also discuss variations within critical policy approaches and position myself in this field. In an appendix to chapter 2 I sketch out steps involved in conducting a critical policy study. While this discussion may be of particular interest to students and other scholars new to policy research, it will hopefully provide all readers with a general understanding of how the critical policy researchers referenced in this book, including me, conduct their work.

In chapter 3, I focus on three policies that encourage and enable private money to enter public schools and districts: school fundraising, student fees, and international education. I examine how these policies and their associated practices impact various groups of students, families, and educators differently. I highlight how they undermine the commitments to equal access to opportunities, equity, open decision-making processes, and prioritizing the public that are foundational to the public school ideal.

Next, in chapter 4, I examine how policies and private resources interact to enable some kids, usually those from advantaged backgrounds, to accumulate more private benefits from public education systems than many of their peers. I show that most school choice policies disproportionately benefit white and affluent kids by providing them access to special learning opportunities not accessible to everyone. I then consider ways parents use their private resources to pay for services outside of schools that give their children advantages inside them; these practices include paying for private psychological testing, purchasing individual course credits from private schools, and sending their kids to private tutoring services.

In the final chapter I present ideas for how readers can participate in debates over privatization and in the fight for strong public education. I suggest sources of information readers can refer to, including research and other publications by public education advocacy groups across the country. I restate the central questions of critical policy analysis and encourage you to ask them of new and existing education policies and practices. I also remind you of what (and who) you are up against in the fight against education privatization. I conclude by arguing, once again, that if we want to live in a society that believes everyone is entitled to the benefits of education, one where very different people live together respectfully and peacefully, and where citizens care about the well-being of others and think critically about the world, then we need the *public school ideal*.

chapter two

Researching Education Privatization: Traditional and Critical Approaches

In 2017, at the request of Ontario's premier and Ministry of Education, the government's education advisors reviewed assessment and report-ing in the province, including the work of the Education Quality and Accountability Office (EQAO) and the standardized tests it adminis-ters to students in grades 3, 6, 9, and 10.[1] The advisors gathered the public's feedback through meetings, webinars, and an online survey. They also met with education stakeholder organizations and various government ministries and directorates and received forty-four written submissions. The advisors consulted experts and commissioned a scan of assessment practices across Canada and around the world. Among many findings, the advisors learned that the majority of participants in the online survey, stakeholder sessions, and public meetings did not believe the EQAO assessments were achieving any of their goals. In particular, participants said the EQAO tests failed to ensure equity, recognize each student's experiences and culture, and minimize nega-tive impacts of the tests on students' well-being and learning. Less than a third said the tests achieve the goal of ensuring accountability on the performance and quality of schools, school boards, and Ontario's pub-licly funded education system – the primary rationale for the creation of the EQAO. In its final report, the advisors identified thirteen areas for improvement and made eighteen recommendations, including the recommendation to redesign provincial large-scale assessments so as to modernize grade 6 assessments of literacy and numeracy, implement a new grade 10 assessment of knowledge, skills, and competences, and phase out the current grades 3 and 9 EQAO assessments and the On-tario Secondary School Literacy Test.

Laura-Lee Kearns interviewed sixteen young people who failed EQAO's grade 10 literacy test to learn about the impacts of their experience of fail-ure.[2] The youth lived in areas with high levels of poverty and most were racialized and/or first generation Canadians. The youth reported feeling shocked when they failed as well as "degraded, humiliated, stressed, and shamed by the test results."[3] Some students second-guessed their abilities and whether they belonged in the courses they were taking, and some attributed their failure to their status as English Language Learners. Many said the tests were unhelpful and worried their futures were now in jeopardy. Kearns concludes, "If the goals of literacy are to promote the well-being of youth, to help youth thrive, and to promote equity within the educational system, then the approach to working with and for diverse and marginalized youth must be rethought."[4]

Hanna Wickstrom, Ellen Fesseha, and Eunice Eunhee Jang investigated the relationship between elementary students with individualized edu-cation plans (IEPs), testing accommodations, and achievement on On-tario's EQAO math test in grade 6.[5] They found that students who had testing accommodations in grade 3 and those who had IEPs at some point between grades 3 and 6 were more likely to show a decline in their math-ematics test scores in grade 6 than students who did not have an IEP or testing accommodations. The investigators conclude that "much more must be done to support learners with special education needs in Ontar-io's EQAO mathematics testing."[6]

The researchers quoted above all examined Ontario's EQAO and its standardized tests, yet their studies reflect different assump-tions and purposes of policy research. The first study was com-missioned by the government, which was interested in evaluating whether EQAO was achieving its goals, while the second was con-ducted by a university-based researcher interested in how failing a test impacted students from marginalized groups. The authors of the third study assumed relationships between parts of the so-cial world are measurable and predictable, while the author of the second study uses a methodology that assumes the opposite.

Two studies call for changes and improvements to EQAO's assessments, while the third advocates for a total rethink, including the possibility of "completely different alternatives and practices to high-stakes, standardized literacy testing."[7] How is it that these three studies – with their different purposes, methods, and assumptions – can all be considered policy research?

In this chapter I describe and compare two general approaches to conceptualizing and studying policy using studies of standardized testing as illustrative examples. Large-scale standardized assessments of student achievement, such as those administered in Ontario by EQAO, represent a form of performance-based accountability transferred from the private sector in education systems across the country.[8] Each of the two general approaches is based on a set of beliefs about the nature of the social world and the purposes of policy research. My goals with this discussion are, first, to introduce you to a variety of ways that any policy, including those that facilitate education privatization, can be investigated and, second, to let you know how I position myself as a critical policy researcher. This chapter may not interest every reader, and you should feel free to skip it if you aren't interested in policy theory. Seasoned scholars may find my descriptions and comparisons oversimplified and incomplete because, as they know, there is a lot of diversity in policy theories and scholarship. If you want to read a more detailed analysis of the histories, theories, and distinctions between different orientations towards education policy I recommend you check out the introductory chapters of *Re-reading Education Policies: A Handbook Studying the Policy Agenda of the 21st Century* by Maarten Simons, Mark Olssen, and Michael Peters.[9] Finally, see the appendix, if you would like to learn about the steps involved in conducting a critical policy research study.

Traditional and Critical Approaches to Policy Analysis

While there are various ways to define and study policy, they can be grouped into two general approaches, or orientations,[10] to policy research based on their common underlying assumptions. Scholars refer to one group variously as including "traditional," "technical-empiricist," or "rational scientific" approaches.[11] The second group includes frameworks characterized by their critical orientation. To be clear, there are a wide variety of theories *within* each of these two approaches. My purpose here is to describe what each group has in common and explain how they differ from each other.

Maarten Simons, Mark Olssen, and Michael Peters explain that traditional approaches share an interest in problem solving. They emerged from a desire to take politics out of decision-making and the belief that specialist knowledge can inform policy decisions. It is these decisions, typically written down in a formal document, that people working within traditional approaches think of as "policy." Traditional approaches view policymakers as (ideally) rational actors who make choices using a rational decision-making process. According to Deborah Stone, this process has five steps: choosing objectives; identifying alternatives; predicting impacts of various options; evaluating possible consequences of each alternative; and finally, choosing the option that will maximize the achievement of objectives with the least cost.[12] This decision-making process is supposedly efficient, systematic, and objective. The decision makers themselves are normally assumed to be government officials or other people in authoritative positions (e.g., school trustees, school and district administrators).

It's common to think and talk about stages in a policy process or cycle. While theorists debate how many stages there are, whether they are linear or not, and what takes place in each one, Werner Jann and Kai Wegrich identify four stages conventionally used in (traditional) policy studies.[13] The first stage, they explain, is agenda setting: A social problem is recognized by policymakers, and they agree to consider different ways it might be addressed. That is, consideration of the problem is on the "agenda" of policymakers. Notably, policymakers view the "problem" as an objective phenomenon. While they may debate its meaning or severity, they view it as actually existing in the world rather than as a situation constructed as a problem by people.

The second stage includes two activities: policy formulation and decision-making. It is here that the rational decision-making process described above comes into play. Policy goals are established, and policy researchers advise decision makers about the costs and benefits of various ways to achieve them. Indeed, this is a key purpose of policy research in traditional approaches: to inform policy decisions. Research is done by researchers inside the government (or governing body) as well as outside it in universities, think tanks, and other organizations. Environmental scans of how other jurisdictions are addressing the problem and formal consultations on policy options are examples of this kind of work. In addition to research, a lot of informal negotiation between public and private actors (e.g., interest groups, government departments, members from different political parties) happens at this time. This stage ends when policymakers make a formal decision.

Next in the process is the implementation stage. At this point, people other than policymakers put the policy into action. According to Jann and Wegrich, implementers ideally receive specific information about how the policy should be carried out and by whom, the resources allocated to its implementation, and how decisions should be made. In elementary and secondary schools, these people include school district leaders, principals and vice principals, teachers, school council chairs, and many others. They might receive a lot or very little guidance from the government or other governing body (e.g., a school board), depending on the policy.

The last stage is evaluation (and possible termination). This is the point at which assessors determine whether the goals of the policy have been achieved. They may also examine other outcomes, intended and otherwise. The review of Ontario's EQAO described in this chapter's opening is an example of research at this stage. Researchers may be external or internal to the government or organization. Their findings are used to inform decisions about whether to maintain, modify, or discontinue the policy.

In addition to conducting research to inform decision makers, many academic researchers study and theorize what happens at each stage. Implementation research, for example, aims to explain how people, places, and policies, as well as interactions between them, impact how a policy is implemented. The "essential implementation question … ," according to policy scholar Meredith

Honig, "is what is implementable and what works for whom, where, when, and why?"[14] In efforts to answer this question researchers consider not only who is involved in implementation but also how their roles, identities, and relationships affect the process. Scholars also try to identify strategies and tools that encourage people to behave in ways that align with policy expectations.[15] A lot of implementation research reflects the traditional approach's underlying belief in the predictability of human behaviour and the social world. Researchers may look for relationships between practices or groups of people to explain policy outcomes. The study of the relationship between students with IEPs, testing accommodations, and students' performance on EQAO's grade 6 math test that I described in this chapter's opening is an example of this kind of study.

While the idea that a policy passes through the stages outlined above remains popular outside academia, scholars both outside and within traditional approaches have offered many critiques of it. I review a few here. First, as I alluded to above, many researchers have shown that the stages are not discrete nor do they necessarily follow one after the other.[16] The model doesn't explain how activities in one stage impact what happens in the others. It adopts a "top-down" perspective that implies policy processes are initiated by privileged institutions (e.g., governments) and fails to recognize policy processes that begin locally (i.e., "bottom-up"). It also focusses on the trajectory of a single policy; it doesn't consider how multiple policies develop alongside and interact with each other. Furthermore, the model ignores other important aspects of policy processes, such as the role of symbols and argumentation.[17] Researchers have also demonstrated that the process is highly political. For example, policy actors work hard to impact what policymakers pay attention to during the problem-recognition and agenda-setting stages; and a lot of bargaining takes place between actors competing for influence during the policy-formulation stage. Some critics say the model is too simplistic and fails to capture the "messy realities" of policy processes.[18] Despite these and other critiques, the idea that policy involves various stages is commonplace.

To summarize, traditional approaches to policy analysis are generally concerned with problem solving. They assume that people are rational beings and that the social world is predictable and knowable through research. The main purposes of research are to inform policy decisions, to describe what happens at various points in a policy process, and to explain policy outcomes.

Critical approaches, while diverse, share some concerns that distinguish them from traditional approaches. Perhaps most significantly, critical policy researchers are interested in understanding how policies create, perpetuate, and/or challenge unequal social relations.[19] Rejecting the ideal of rational and objective policy processes, we recognize that these processes are inherently political because they involve people making choices that benefit some groups while disadvantaging others. Thus, critical policy researchers seek to identify policy "winners" and "losers."[20] Laura-Lee Kearns's study of the impact of failing EQAO's grade 10 literacy test for marginalized youth (described at the beginning of this chapter) is an example of this kind of work. Unlike traditional researchers who may strive to remain neutral, critical policy researchers view their work politically and see it as part of struggles to create a more socially just world.

Critical policy researchers are also interested in how power circulates throughout policy processes. For example, they might ask, *Who participated in the creation of a policy?* or *Whose interests are reflected in this policy document and whose are absent?* They will likely consider the involvement of international organizations, foundations, and businesses on public education policy. Alternatively, critical policy researchers might investigate how actors have tried to resist or change policies that create inequalities. Stephanie Schroeder, Elizabeth Currin, and Todd McCardle, for example, studied how mothers in the advocacy group Opt Out Florida turned to Facebook to "learn, share, organise, and act" in their efforts to resist the harms of standardized testing.[21]

Critical policy researchers also pay close attention to context. On one hand, we are interested in situating policies within their broader social and historical contexts. We try to answer questions such as *Why this policy now?* and *How has this support for this policy endured?* Scholar Laura Pinto's socio-historical account of standard-ized assessments for students in grades, 3, 6, 9, and 10 in Ontario, for example, points to middling public satisfaction with Ontario's public schools and a 1995 Royal Commission Report, *For the Love of Learning,* which recommended some testing, as helping to set the stage for the introduction of the province's first large-scale stu-dent assessment program in 1997.[22] Despite opposition by teacher unions and some parents and researchers, Ontario's assessments carry on, in part due to the continued support of the PC, NDP, and Liberal parties.[23]

At the same time, critical policy researchers recognize that a pol-icy's various contexts – historical, geographical, political, cultural, economic, material – influence how it is understood, debated, and taken up (or not). This point has important implications for poli-cymakers who aim to identify a policy that is achieving its goals in one place, attempt to replicate it in other places, and expect to achieve similar results in these new sites. This is not to say that a policy that works in one place cannot be effective somewhere else; rather, the point is that replication cannot be assumed or assured. Instead of looking for "what went wrong" when a policy doesn't achieve expected outcomes, critical policy researchers often exam-ine its contexts to understand why it unfolded as it did.

Researchers Goli Rezai-Rashti and Allison Segeren, for example, examined how local and provincial policy contexts impact school leaders' enactment of accountability policies, including standard-ized testing.[24] They interviewed eighteen leaders in high schools in Toronto, Ontario, and Vancouver, BC, and compared their ex-periences. School leaders in Ontario reported feeling tremendous pressure from their school district and the Ministry of Education to produce high test scores. They explained that schools with low scores may be called to account for their results and put under greater surveillance: for example, these schools might be assigned coaches from the ministry or school district to oversee improve-ment efforts. And, like all schools, they have to submit School Improvement Plans for district approval that detail how they will improve student achievement. In response to the pressure to produce high scores, Ontario leaders said they might encourage students expected to perform poorly to stay home on test days, place them in lower-level academic tracks that are not tested at all, defer their tests, or, in the case of the grade 10 literacy test, place students directly into the alternative literacy course (an option supposedly only for students who previously failed the test twice). Leaders in BC, however, reported that they sensed a movement away from provincial standardized testing and hence did not feel the pressure to produce results as their peers did in Ontario. Thus, they did not engage in strategies to raise their schools' scores. Instead, they criticized the tests outright.

However, leaders in both provinces said that the publication of school test scores on websites and in media and other reports influences their work. Schools with lower scores, especially those in racially diverse, low income neighbourhoods, are further stigmatized by the reports. Leaders said that some parents, particularly those in middle-class families, use test scores to compare and select schools for their children. Thus leaders, especially in schools with low scores, engage in efforts to market their schools to attract parents and recruit and retain students, raise scores, and avoid being closed due to low enrolment. Rezai-Rashti and Segeren point out that leaders' efforts to manage their test results and sell their schools mean they have less time and money to spend on improving instruction and addressing equity and social justice issues.

In summary then, Rezai-Rashti and Segeren's study shows the significance of policy context on leaders' behaviours. In Ontario, where pressure from the district and province to perform is high, leaders strategize to produce higher scores for their schools. In BC, where the pressure is lower, leaders engage in critique. However, all report engaging in marketing and promotion efforts as an outcome of the publication of standardized test scores. This work is especially important in schools in racialized and low income communities.

Many researchers with a critical orientation towards policy are interested in language. Some might focus on what a policy text says, whereas others are interested in how people use language to persuade others to understand the world as they do. In fact, policy debates are often arguments over the meaning of a social situation, and much policy advocacy is about trying to convince other people to see an issue in a particular way. A critically oriented policy researcher might, for example, examine the different arguments mobilized in support of and in opposition to standard testing. I should point out that some traditional policy researchers are also interested in language. They may consider how language is used to describe or "frame" a problem, but they might not examine its effects on social inequalities and power relations.

Beyond these shared interests, critical policy researchers are a diverse group. First, they come from a range of disciplines, including sociology, political science, anthropology, history, educational administration, and the politics of education. Key interests, theories, and methodologies that characterize various disciplines are reflected in their critical policy work. For example, researchers from anthropology may be more inclined to see policy as a cultural practice and use ethnography as their methodology. Historians, on the other hand, may be more likely to examine documents and construct accounts of what happened in the past.

Second, while many critical policy researchers are interested in what I described above as the implementation stage of a linear policy process, some have tried to think differently from researchers grounded in traditional approaches about what happens when official policies meet local contexts. For example, Bradley Levinson, Margaret Sutton, and Teresa Winstead offer the concept of policy appropriation.[25] This concept refers to the ways that people in local sites (such as schools) interpret official, external policies and make sense of them within their own context. This concept recognizes local actors as creative agents in policy processes. So, too, does Annette Braun, Stephen Ball, Meg Maguire, and Kate Hoskins' concept of policy enactment. According to these researchers, enactment "involves creative processes of interpretation and translation" as people read, write, and talk about what official policies mean for them and their workplaces.[26] The study I described above by Rezai-Rashti and Segeren is an example of school leaders' policy enactment of standardized testing.

Third, some critical policy researchers adopt narrow definitions of policy whereas others define it much more broadly. There are those who, like researchers in the traditional approach, see policy as formal decisions of government or other authoritative bodies. They limit their study of policy to texts that document these decisions; Levinson, Sutton, and Winstead refer to these policies as "authorized" policies.[27] Other researchers consider policy to include documents created to support formal policy decisions or related to a particular issue. These texts may include "unauthorized" or "informal" policies that are produced by individuals in response to government or school board decisions.[28] Some policy researchers define policy as what people actually *do* (as opposed to what they are instructed to do).

Still other critical policy researchers define policy as discourse. From this perspective, language is more than just a way to represent meaning: it creates and recreates the social world. Rather than viewing a policy text as simply a statement about a decision or a set of instructions, researchers who define policy as discourse may study how policy creates problems, solutions, and subjects. For example, Cameron Graham and Dean Neu, drawing on theorist Michel Foucault and focusing on standardized testing in Alberta, explain that examinations are a technique used by governments to make individuals – and populations – governable.[29] When a student takes a test, select aspects of who they are are made visible and are subject to evaluations, comparisons, classifications, rankings, and measurements by others. The tests encourage students to behave in ways that will produce socially desirable results, and students deemed low (or high) performing may internalize these judgments and reproduce them in future behaviour. Individual students' test scores are aggregated to the school, district, and provincial levels, and consequently, impact the behaviour of teachers, administrators, trustees, and even taxpayers. Teachers in schools with "bad" results may be pressured to changed their practices, while administrators may refer to their schools' good results when recruiting. Parents may use test scores to select schools for their children. Graham and Neu argue that standardized tests encourage all these actors to self-regulate according to social norms and actively construct themselves as subjects.[30]

Richard Bowe, Stephen Ball, and Anne Gold propose the broad concept of a continuous policy cycle that includes policy decisions, discourses, struggles for influence, and enactment.[31] They explain that policy activity takes place across three interrelated contexts: the context of influence, the context of text production, and the context of practice. The context of influence is where formal policies are established. Here people develop policy ideas, struggle over their meanings, and create discourses. These activities take place publicly, including in the media and formal consultations, and behind closed doors. The context of text production includes texts representing policy decisions and their meanings. They are written for broad audiences and include government policy documents, legislation, speeches, websites, media releases, reports, and research. These documents are the outcomes of negotiations and compromises. And, since texts are produced by different people over time, they may contradict each other. Finally, the third context, that of practice, is the arena that policy addresses (e.g., schools). It is here where people interpret policy texts and figure out how they will change their practices to align with their interpretations, if at all. Research on standardized assessment policy might focus on one or more of these policy contexts.

The next two chapters contain findings from critical analyses of policies – formal and informal – that enable some children to benefit from public education in ways that others cannot. Specifically, in the next chapter I focus on three endogenous privatization policies that call parents to participate as funders of public education: school fundraising, school fees, and international education. I show that these policies' winners are often white and/or affluent students and their families, whereas their losers are more often students who are poor, Indigenous, racialized, and/or have special needs.

chapter three

Funding Advantage in Public Schools

One summer I received a letter from my sons' high school. Among details about the first day of class, the Guidance Office's summer hours, and a new daily schedule, it included instructions about registration. It asked parents to complete a set of forms that students should bring to the school on registration day, when they would also receive their locker assignment, lock, agenda, and timetable. Additionally, parents were asked to select and pay for a yearbook ($35), athletics T-shirt ($10); agenda ($5), and student activity fee ($35) using SchoolCash Online. The letter explained that the student activity fee "is directed to student leadership and co-curricular activities including: clubs, teams, student leadership councils and special student events." Parents were told that their "support is appreciated."

As a parent I wondered, again, whether or not to pay the fees. While I didn't think my kids needed any more T-shirts or that they would use agendas (!), I didn't wanted them to miss out on getting a yearbook, especially since one of them was graduating that year. The requested $35 student activity fee was trickier: I know these fees pay for activities I think are important for all kids, and I know education funding to schools doesn't cover their costs. My sons play on a bunch of sports teams and participate in various clubs – aren't I obligated then to pay the activity fee? But what about the kids whose families can't afford it?

After mulling it over and talking to my boys, I signed on to School-Cash Online as directed in the letter. SchoolCash Online is a website that enables parents to pay for school expenses online using their credit or bank cards. It was introduced in my school district amid some mild controversy over the fact that the company that runs SchoolCash Online charges a fee for every transaction. But of course they do; how else could the business be profitable?

I found the items listed on the site and noted that beside each one was the word "optional" to indicate, one would think, that the fee was voluntary. I paid the $35 activity fee and, unsure how the school would know I'd paid, I printed out the receipt.

On the designated day in August, a week before the first day of class, I took one of my sons to the school. I waited as he went to the office to hand in his registration forms and pick up his timetable. When he came back to the car he was fuming.

"Mom," he said, "you have to go in there. The office is telling kids they can't get their timetables until they pay their fees online and bring in the receipt. They're not allowed to do that, right?"

Of course he was right. I know from my research that all school fees in Ontario are optional. But what could I do? I didn't believe that marching into the office and telling the staff to stop doing what they were doing would do much to change the situation or help my sons' (or my) relationship with the school. In fact, my son later confessed that he had called the office himself from inside the school to tell the person on the other line that they should not be denying kids their timetables because they hadn't paid fees. It didn't help.

That night, I tweeted the following:

Sue Winton @Swintoncpa
Quick follow-up to my article below: Kids at my sons' school are currently being denied their timetables for not showing proof they've paid their optional fees @tdsb @BPCIguidance @ ParthiKandavel

I copied my sons' school, school board, and trustee. The school board responded:

Toronto District School Board @tdsb
Replying to @Swintoncpa @BPCIguidance and @ParthiKandavel
We're sorry to hear about this experience as that shouldn't have been the case. We've followed up with the school and the timetable can be picked up anytime. Please just ask for the Principal.

I wondered why students should have to speak to the principal and how they would know to do so, but I was pleased to get a response from the board. I then heard from the trustee:

Parti Kandavel @ParthiKandavel
Hi Sue @Swintoncpa, just seeing this, very sorry to hear this happened. I spoke with Superintendent, Peter Chang, @pctdsb, he's assured me it was an office mistake that should not have happened. Pls assure your son and other kids, this will not be happening. Pls contact if not [sic]

An office mistake? An isolated incident? While we all slip up, I had my doubts.

Just a few days later I received a note from another son's school, which read, "PLEASE NOTE: Any student who is unable to attend the registration process on August 28th or 29th must pick up his/her timetable and pay the $75.00 student activity fee on September 3rd in the Cafeteria." Here's what I tweeted about it:

Sue Winton @Swintoncpa
Another son, another @tdsb high school, another expectation parents pay optional fees @aarts_michelle @malvernci_TDSB

The trustee replied:

Michelle Aarts, TDSB @aarts_michelle
Fees are actually optional but I know the language in notices does not always reflect the optional part. I will ask the Superintendents to review school notices.

I'm not confident it won't happen again.

Raising money for public education is nothing new. Parents have organized fun fairs, students have sold lottery tickets, and teachers have collected money for class trips for decades, if not longer. What is new, however, is the intensity of fundraising efforts in schools today. If you're a parent with a child in elementary school in Canada, chances are good that you've bought cookies

or brownies at a school event, perhaps you even baked (or purchased) them before they were sold (back) to you. Maybe you
paid for your high schooler's agenda or team uniform, or perhaps
your child attends one of the growing number of specialty programs offered by public schools, such as exceptional athlete, arts,
or the International Baccalaureate programs. School districts also
try to top up public funding, and many are now looking beyond
Canada's borders for revenue sources. In this chapter I examine
how private money enters public schools and districts via school
fundraising, student fees, and international student tuition. I also
consider how these practices impact various groups of students,
families, and educators differently. Finally, I highlight how they
undermine the commitments to equal access to opportunities, equity, open decision-making processes, and prioritizing the public,
which are foundational to the public education ideal outlined in
the first chapter.

Fundraising

Walking around my neighbourhood in June, it seems that every
elementary school I pass is either advertising an upcoming car-
nival or thanking its business sponsors. While not every school
hosts these end-of-year events, many schools across the country
are involved in fundraising at some point in the year. According
to a 2019 survey of 1,254 public schools conducted by People for
Education, an education advocacy group in Ontario, 99 per cent of
elementary and 89 per cent of secondary schools in the province
fundraise.[1] While recent statistics are unavailable for other provinces and the territories, a 2006 study sponsored by the Canadian
Teachers' Federation, the Canadian Centre for Policy Alternatives,
and the Fédération des syndicats de l'enseignement concluded
that the practice was widespread across the country.[2] A plethora
of news articles and a cursory review of government websites confirm this remains true today.

Administrators, teachers, and other staff fundraise in almost
all schools. Parents, caregivers, and other community members

also lead school fundraising activities in many places. They may do so as members of school councils, home and school associations, parent advisory councils, or fundraising associations set up exclusively to raise money for a school. A 2016 survey in Ontario's Toronto District School Board (TDSB) found that 86 per cent of school councils fundraise and that it's one of their most common activities.[3]

School fundraisers, whether parents or school staff, raise money in a variety of ways. A popular strategy is to sell goods such as books, cookie dough, wrapping paper, magazines, and pizza. The popularity of food sales as fundraisers in particular is evident in resistance to various provinces' efforts to restrict the availability of unhealthy food in schools. When New Brunswick revised its policy to ban the "sale of foods and beverages with lower nutritional value in fundraising activities organized by, through or for schools/students," for example, pushback was swift.[4] A parent in one school's home and school association lamented the new policy since its Halloween event, which involved candy, raised half of the group's annual fundraising dollars. "It's the children who are going to suffer," she said. A second organization was forced to rethink its "Popsicles on the playground" initiative. Parents in both groups expressed support for healthier options but were worried about how the policy changes would impact fundraising. A similar situation arose in Ontario when its government banned the sale of foods containing high levels of sugar, fat, and sodium in schools in 2010. Ontario's policy, however, allows ten exceptions per year, thus enabling fundraising through pizza lunches and sales of other foods not typically permitted.

Events such as fun fairs, movie nights, and parties for parents are also common fundraising initiatives. These activities generate money through ticket sales, games, auctions, and/or food and beverage sales. In Alberta, fundraising associations can also raise money through charity casinos. These events are particularly lucrative as a school can raise more than $60,000 in just one night.[5] However, casinos require volunteers from the school to assist at the event, and not all schools can get this number of volunteers to come out. The importance of casinos to school fundraising efforts became particularly apparent when the Catholic Archdiocese of Edmonton banned Edmonton's Catholic schools from using them as a way to raise money. A parent explained, "It's going to come out of our pockets, or the kids are going to lack in their education ... If they don't let us do casinos ... I mean, you can only sell so many chocolates."[6] Fundraising events sometimes involve sponsorships in which businesses give schools or fundraising groups money in exchange for promoting their product or service at the event.

Funds for schools may also be generated through grants offered by businesses, civil-society organizations, and governments. People for Education found in 2019 that 75 per cent of elementary and 83 per cent of secondary schools surveyed received grants.[7] Of these secondary schools, 24 per cent of the grants were awarded by businesses, 30 per cent by philanthropies, and 82 per cent by the government. For elementary schools, these figures are 17 per cent, 18 per cent and 61 per cent respectively. One problem with turning to grants is that the funder typically decides how the money can be used. If your school needs new instruments but a particular grant funds only playgrounds, you're out of luck. A second problem with grants is that the funding may be a one-time-only award. If a school's needs are ongoing, then new funding sources have to be identified each year. Of course, writing successful grants also takes time and skills, including facility with English or French, knowledge of budgets, and persuasive writing. Some schools may have parents with these skills, but others don't. In these cases, administrators and teachers do this work.

Fundraisers may also seek donations from parents, philanthropists, businesses, or the general public. A parent advisory council in a Vancouver suburb, for example, runs a "Kick Start Campaign" each fall that asks parents to make a cash donation. Its 2018–19 campaign raised $15,770.[8] The money was supposed to fund speakers, classroom budgets, workshops, and art supplies.

Some teachers appeal to potential donors online. A secondary school teacher in Nunavut, for example, set up a campaign on GoFundMe.com (a website for crowdsourcing) to raise money to buy a greenhouse where he and his students could grow vegetables.[9] He asked for $4,500 and ultimately raised more than four times as much. In addition, WeldCor, a welding-equipment company, donated two additional greenhouses, and Loblaw gave them seed kits. A grade one teacher in Vancouver also turned to crowdsourcing and raised almost $2,100 for healthy snacks, winter clothing, toys, and other classroom supplies.[10] The #clearthelists Canada campaign invites teachers to post their classroom wish lists and asks members of the public to fund them. In the United States, the lists are posted directly on Amazon. Further, celebrities, including Kristen Bell and Busy Philipps, feature teachers' pleas for support via Twitter (e.g., see #10FeaturedTeachers).

Perhaps we should not be surprised by teachers' appeals for assistance. A Saskatchewan Teachers' Federation survey of its members found that 96 per cent of respondents spend their own money on resources for their classrooms,[11] while the Nova Scotia Teachers Union estimates that teachers spend an average of $525 of their own money on supplies each year.[12] This practice is formally recognized by the federal government. Teachers in Canada can claim up to $1,000 for teaching-supply expenses on their federal taxes.

Fundraising is a lot of work and takes a lot of time. A mother who organizes the Scholastic book fair at her children's school told me, "These roles, they are very, very demanding, like incredibly demanding, like I cannot tell you how many hours I've clocked in … it's during the day, it's, it's not like someone could take off work and say 'I'm sorry I'm volunteering.'" Administrators, teachers and staff who organize fundraisers do so in addition to their regular work. The time they spend collating pizza orders, looking for donations, or completing grant applications is time that they could have spent planning lessons, talking to parents and students, or reading up on new ideas for the classroom.

Fundraising Policies

Despite its prevalence across the country, only a handful of governments have policies or guidelines that address school fundraising: New Brunswick, Ontario, Yukon, and Manitoba. These policies vary in terms of scope and detail. In other provinces, government endorsements of fundraising sometimes show up in other policies. Nova Scotia's *Food and Nutrition Policy for Nova Scotia Public Schools*, for example, states, "Fundraising contributes valuable educational programs and opportunities for students."[13] Support for school fundraising in Newfoundland and Labrador is evident in its Schools Act in references to the responsibilities of school councils and in its handbook for school councils.[14]

New Brunswick's *Contributions of Resources by Parents Policy 132*, the Yukon's *Fund Raising in Schools* Policy, and Ontario's *Fundraising Guideline* outline acceptable uses of fundraised dollars. New Brunswick's policy permits schools and districts to fundraise for "activities that supplement the prescribed educational program," including extra- and co-curricular activities.[15] It states that parents cannot be asked to fundraise (or pay fees) to cover costs associated with providing "the prescribed educational program," including textbooks, or materials related to the "programs, goods and services that are fundamental to a pupil's education."[16] New Brunswick's policy applies only to the province's schools and school districts, not to organizations or groups that volunteer to raise money for public schools (e.g., home and school associations). Similarly, in Ontario, the province's *Fundraising Guideline* states, "Funds raised for school purposes are used to complement, not replace, public funding for education,"[17] and it provides some examples of acceptable and unacceptable uses of monies generated through fundraising. Unacceptable uses include purchasing classroom-learning materials; textbooks; and facility upgrades, renewal, or maintenance funded by government grants. However, fundraised monies can be used for "[s]upplies, equipment or services which complement items funded by provincial grants."[18] Forty-three per cent of elementary schools participating in People for Education's 2019 survey reported they fundraise for classroom materials, while 68 per cent raise money for technology, 52 per cent fundraise for their libraries, and half report using fundraised dollars to support the arts.[19] Before the COVID-19 pandemic, many people argued that technology, library books, and art supplies were not "complementary" but necessary for a well-rounded education. When schools closed during the pandemic, student access to technology was critically important, and school districts across Ontario struggled to ensure students had devices and Internet connection.

The Yukon's fundraising policy is more general. It states that fundraisers should "benefit students; enhance the quality of education in the schools; and/or contribute to the development of students as responsible citizens."[20] It does not specify what can and cannot be purchased with fundraised dollars. Manitoba's policy is the briefest of the four provinces' policies and focuses on financial reporting of school-generated funds. Rather than identifying acceptable use of those funds, it suggests school boards create policies that outline allowable expenditures. Indeed, school boards across the country have fundraising policies, even in the absence of provincial directives.

How Much?

The total amount of money raised through school fundraising across Canada is unknown. Provinces and territories have different expectations and procedures for reporting how much is raised. In Ontario, boards are required to include consolidated amounts fundraised in their annual financial statements. While the figures are publicly available, they include multiple sources of funding (grant awards, vendor or photographer commissions, and a variety of fees) in addition to funds raised by school councils. Based on the audited financial statements of Ontario's seventy-two school boards, People for Education reports that schools generated more than 583 million dollars in 2018.[21] Taking a different approach, *Toronto Star* journalist Patty Winsa looked at the average amount of school-generated funds raised per elementary student in 2012–13 in English school boards in the Greater Toronto Area. Relying on the boards' reports, she found substantial differences in the amounts they raised. York Catholic District School Board, for example, raised about $358 per elementary student while the TDSB, the board directly south of York Catholic (literally *across the street*) raised an average of just $118.10 per student.[22] What's more, the Toronto Catholic District School Board (TCDSB) raised an average of $233.99 per student. That's nearly double the amount raised by the TDSB, a board in the *very same city*.

A unique TDSB 2017 report provides important information about differences between schools within a single board. It includes the amounts that both a school and its school council raised in 2016–17. It shows that some schools raised around $1,000 that year while others raised more than fifteen times that amount.[23] Similarly, some school councils didn't raise anything at all, while a handful raised more than $100,000 – one even pulled in close to $300,000. Schools vary in size, of course, and schools with fewer students might be expected to raise less money than larger ones. Thus, a key figure is the amount raised per student. The TDSB's 2017 report shows that this amount varies by hundreds of dollars.

Differences in amounts raised arise largely because not all communities can afford to give money to their schools. Patty Winsa mapped the amount of school-generated funds raised per student in TDSB's elementary schools in 2012–13. The map shows that the schools that raise the most money are typically located in high income neighbourhoods, while schools raising less are, not surprisingly, located in low income neighbourhoods.[24] Speaking about fundraising in his board, an Ontario principal remarked, "Through school fundraising the rich kids are maintaining a level that they are already getting at home."[25]

Importantly, the gap between schools that can and cannot fundraise has increased over time. Based on its findings from its annual surveys, People for Education reports that in 2008 for every $1 raised by lowest 10 per cent of fundraising schools in Ontario, the top 10 per cent of fundraising schools raised $25. By 2017, the ratio had almost doubled: for every $1 raised by the lowest fundraising schools the top 10 per cent raised $49.[26] Regional differences also exist. People for Education's 2017 survey of schools found that elementary schools in central Ontario raised a median amount of $10,000, while schools in Northern Ontario raised just half that amount.

Fundraising advocates sometimes point out that schools in poorer communities qualify for more grants than affluent schools, and thus they have resources to tap into that make up any differences created by fundraising.[27] Indeed, the TDSB's 2017 report I referred to above might be used to challenge the idea that differences in school-generated funds matter. In addition to showing how much money schools bring in from external sources, it identifies various grants and other additional government funding that some schools receive based on measures of external challenges affecting student success. Based on these measures, schools are ranked from highest to lowest need in a learning opportunity index (LOI). The report suggests that when total school funding is taken into account (including school-generated funds, donations, and grants that top up school budgets), the differences in the per-pupil amount received by schools with different LOI scores is minimal. So does this mean fundraising doesn't really make a difference in TDSB schools? Not necessarily. The grants and additional funding schools receive normally come with restrictions on how they can be spent, while fundraised dollars can be spent on anything that "enhance[s] the school program and support[s] school initiatives," according to the TDSB's fundraising policy.[28] Further, some schools receive grants to pay for food or activities that other schools count on parents to provide, thus freeing up money to be spent elsewhere. Finally, a 2017 report by Toronto Social Planning showed that the board spent just over half of provincial funds allocated to support students who are at a greater risk of poor academic achievement for this purpose.[29] The board used the rest to pay other bills.

Why Fundraise?

A parent I interviewed for a study in Ontario explained why she participates in fundraising initiatives at her school:

> The government doesn't supply enough funding for schools ... Like our kids don't even have textbooks, okay? I find that appalling. It's photocopied sheets and papers ... and it's all "sorry, there's no money. there's no money. there's no money" ... this is why we fundraise.

This parent is not alone in her belief that Ontario's public schools are not funded adequately. In Ontario, many educators, parents, and advocates for more public funds point to changes introduced in the Education Quality Improvement Act in 1997 for leaving the province's public schools underfunded and putting new demands on parents to fundraise. In 2000, for example, former Ontario Premier Kathleen Wynne, then a member of the Metro Parents Network, argued that parents "can't sell enough muffins to make up the gap."[30] Similarly in Alberta in 2004, then Liberal education critic Don Massey blamed "10 years of chronic underfunding in the public system" for Alberta schools' growing dependence on parent fundraising and volunteerism. Successive governments in Ontario have since adjusted how they determine education funding, but some parents, educators, and critics believe public education in the province remains inadequately funded.[31] So, too, do some Albertans. Fundraising to fill funding gaps will not address the problem it aims to solve, however. Instead, it enables governments to underfund – or many would say *continue* to underfund – public education.

Rather than filling gaps, some advocates view fundraising as a way to enhance the basic educational program available to students. Indeed, this is how fundraising is described in the TDSB's 2017–18 *Fundraising Guide*. This document states that the board believes that "it is not the responsibility of parents or school communities to raise funds for basic educational requirements, but rather that school communities may raise funds to *enhance* programs and support school/student initiatives" [emphasis mine].[32] Fundraised dollars buy a wide range of goods, services, and opportunities, including school supplies, books, musical instruments, technology, sports equipment, swimming pools, artistic performances, gymnasiums, guest speakers, playgrounds, transportation, graduation activities, school trips, and much more. As I've mentioned above, people debate which of these items and activities are actually enhancements rather than essential for learning.

Permitting parents to fundraise for "extras" while it pays for the "basics" enables governments to look as though they are meeting their requirement to ensure all children have free access to education. In fact, they are violating the public school ideal's requirement that governments fully fund public schools so that a family's ability to pay does not impact the quality of education its children receive. Fundraising further violates the public school ideal by creating unequal opportunities for kids to benefit from their public school experiences.

Who Benefits from School Fundraising? Who Loses?

School fundraising is supposed to support students, and many kids do enjoy its benefits. Some fundraisers enable schools to purchase resources that everyone in the school can enjoy, including library books, computers, team uniforms, and band instruments. There are also instances in which fundraising supports only particular grades or groups of students, such as when funds are used to provide snacks, decorations, and music for graduations or to create play spaces for young children too small for the slides and monkey bars in the schoolyard. Fundraisers to build or replace playgrounds are not uncommon, and this kind of initiative expands the potential reach of fundraising since the structures can be used on weekends and after school by other members of the community. In Toronto, extensive fundraising efforts by a not-for-profit organization lead by a local public school principal netted the school and its community a cricket field, batting cages, a multisport court, an outdoor amphitheatre, a butterfly meadow, a digital scoreboard, summer camps, a wide range of recreational programs, and more. But what about the places where school staff and communities can't or don't fundraise? Should the children who attend those schools simply go without?

School fundraising perpetuates inequities in the very spaces intended to address them: public schools. Children in schools that raise more money have access to more opportunities and resources than those in schools that raise less. Often funds come from the families and friends of children in the school, but teachers and administrators sometimes secure the funds.

But unequal access to opportunities and their benefits are not the only problems. Fundraising may come at the cost of building and sustaining inclusive school communities. Inclusive schools are ones in which diversity is embraced and everyone feels safe, accepted, and valued. Kids who cannot contribute to school fundraising initiatives may feel excluded if they are unable to sell wrapping paper to family members or friends, find sponsors for dance-a-thons, or buy books at the book fair. This problem may be exacerbated when schools publicly acknowledge or reward students who sell a specific number of subscriptions or when classes compete to see which one raises the most money.

The issue of exclusion is not limited to students. While governments and other advocates tout fundraising as a great way to get parents involved with their children's school, a study by researcher Linn Posey-Maddox found that a California school council's increased focus on fundraising had a negative impact on some parents' engagement with the school. A mother in her study explained:

> I feel the tenor of the MPTO [PTA] has changed; it seems to be less a place where we all work together for good things for our kids and more about who can plan the most elaborate, biggest fundraiser ... I think the "professionalization" of the volunteerism alienates a lot of the school community; I know it makes me reluctant to continue volunteering.[33]

Posey-Maddox also found that parents may avoid parent-teacher association meetings because of their emphasis on fundraising. One person said,

> The first year was like "we need this, do that, raise this money." It just seemed like, for parents who don't have time nor the money to do it, you start feeling inadequate because you can't be this PTA mom, and doin' all this stuff for the kids ...[34]

Avoiding meetings of school councils or other advisory bodies means these parents miss out on opportunities to participate in decision-making that may impact their children. While they don't always achieve their mandate, advising principals is the main responsibility of mandatory parent organizations in Canadian schools. Parents who participate also get the chance to form relationships with administrators, teachers, and other parents. They can develop social networks that may be useful when they need information or help. Parents who stay away from school councils to avoid fundraising miss out on these opportunities. Furthermore, Posey-Maddox's study showed that parents who did not fundraise felt their non-monetary contributions to the school and their children's education were valued less by school staff than the dollars brought in by fundraising parents.

In another study, Posey-Maddox revealed negative consequences of fundraising for low income and racialized families.[35] She investigated mainly white upper-middle-class parents who choose to send their children to local public schools in Chicago. She interviewed a member of a citywide parent organization and parents of children in five schools that saw a decrease in low income students between 2000–10; four of the schools also saw at least a 10 per cent growth in white student populations. Circumventing established parent-teacher groups such as PTAs, the white upper-middle-class parents set up groups that focused exclusively on fundraising to ensure the schools could provide the programs and resources they desired for their children. They met each other and fundraising parents from other schools in people's homes, online, through a fee-based parent organization, and at a fundraising seminar – spaces not all parents could access. While the fundraising parents espoused commitments to supporting all students in the school, Posey-Maddox found that they rarely sought input from or collaborated with the majority working-class and lower income families. Instead, the fundraising parents assumed that the resources and programs they wanted for their children would be good for the kids from lower income families as well. Alexandra Freidus, who studied white middle-class parents' efforts to improve a public school in a gentrifying neighbourhood in Brooklyn, New York, witnessed something similar: the fundraising parents assumed other parents agreed with their priorities or they simply ignored the wishes of others.[36] This research shows that fundraising can create or exacerbate divisions between different races and classes.

In addition to creating the schools they desire for their children, fundraising serves another purpose for some parents, especially those from the middle class: it enables them to fulfil neoliberal expectations of a good parent. Bronwyn Davies and Peter Bansel explain that neoliberal subjects' "desires, hopes, ideals and fears have been shaped in such a way that they desire to be morally worthy, responsibilized individuals, who, as successful entrepreneurs, can produce the best for themselves and their families."[37] One way they can do so is through raising money that buys their children opportunities. Carol Vincent and Stephen Ball's research in England showed that providing enrichment opportunities to develop all aspects of their children is an aspect of "good parenting" for middle-class parents.[38] Furthermore, participating in fundraising enables parents to demonstrate their good parenting to others – something middle-class parents desire.

School administrators also benefit from fundraising. First, funds generated to supplement school budgets mean principals can offer students more or better materials and opportunities. In provinces and districts with open boundaries and choice programs, additional resources may make a school more attractive to parents and students. The more students that attend a school, the larger the school's budget. The school may also benefit from its reputation as a school of choice. A study by Joseph Di Bona and colleagues in North Carolina showed that more than half of principals would continue to seek additional funds from non-government sources even if the activities these sources fund were fully paid for by tax dollars.[39] This finding, and a similar one by researchers Brian Brent and Stephen Lunden, shows that financial need is not the only reason principals engage in fundraising.[40]

Indeed, a principal in one of my studies made it clear that school leaders benefit politically by permitting fundraising if the school's parent community desires it. When I asked her why she allowed the Scholastic book fair to continue despite her disdain for it, she said, "The parents would call the trustee … 'Oh, Principal Bans Book Fairs.' I can just see it on the cover of the *[Toronto] Star*. No, no, no, no, no." She also explained,

> I have to pick my battles, right? Because I'm going to be the one that says, "No, we're not having a lunch program." I can't say no to everything. So, I have to … so that I will hold my moral ground on a lunch program, but I just have to let it go with the beautiful auction on November 24th,

where they will raise $30,000, and then, um, you know the gym will get stuff, the I guess the Scientist in the Schools will come in, and they'll do field trips for the kids, that kind of stuff.

Of course, governments benefit from fundraising. I've already mentioned a few ways: it absolves them from increasing funding to schools and enables them to look as though they are meeting their legal requirements to provide free access to schooling. Like school administrators, governments benefit politically from fundraising because it secures middle-class parents' support of the public system since they can use it to accrue private benefits for their own children for much less than the cost of an elite private school.

Businesses benefit from their involvement in school fundraisers in a variety of ways as well, depending on how they are involved. If they advertise, hold exclusive sales contracts, sponsor events, or are recognized for donations, businesses gain from the ability to market their products to students and staff in the school. They may also benefit financially if children and their families buy their products or sell them to others. Scholastic Book Fairs and magazine sales are two common examples. The free labour of schools' voluntary salesforces (i.e., parents) is another benefit enjoyed by businesses. Finally, businesses may benefit from developing a reputation as a supporter of public education through their donations of money, materials, and/or labour.

School Fees

In addition to fundraising, private money enters schools through parent fees. While education must be provided free of charge to all resident students of Canada, all provinces and territories permit schools to charge fees for some services, programs, or resources. They vary in terms of what they allow, and the allowances are more or less explicit, depending on the jurisdiction. New Brunswick's Education Act, for example, guarantees "free school privileges" to everyone who is school aged, has not graduated from high school, and is a resident of the province.[41] These privileges include "programs, goods and services that are fundamental to a pupil's education."[42] However, parents are expected to provide materials and supplies for students' personal use (e.g., notebooks, pencils), clothing, and musical instruments if they are required. Manitoba's Public School Fees policy has similar stipulations. It states,

> A school division/district shall not charge fees for goods and services provided to students of school age without which the student could not meet required learning outcomes or assessment requirements of an educational program provided by the division/district except for:
> - materials used in goods that are intended for the student to take home for personal use;
> - the purchase of paper, writing tools, calculators, student planners, exercise books, computer diskettes and other school supplies and equipment for a student's personal use;
> - the rental of a musical instrument for a student's personal use;
> - fees in respect of field trips, team trips or special events to recover associated actual expenses only, including transportation, accommodation, meals, entrance fees and equipment rental but not including substitute teacher costs.[43]

As these policies suggest, there are different types of fees. First, there are the fees that every student in a class, grade, or school is asked to pay. Lord Byng Secondary School in Vancouver, for example, posted its Standard General School Fee Schedule for 2019–20 on its website.[44] It includes two groupings of fees. The first grouping, simply called "Fee Type," lists a student agenda book and student activities/student leadership. These fees total $30 per student. The fee schedule then lists "Optional Fees," including the costs of a yearbook, lock, and various optional gym trips. Some of these fees are particular to specific groups of students, such as a grade 8 camp and costs associated with graduation. Listing these fees under the heading "Optional" suggests that the agenda and student activity fees are required.

Fees like those listed in Lord Byng's Standard General School Fee Schedule are charged in high schools across the country, although their amounts vary a lot. In Ontario, People for Education's

2019 survey of high school principals found that 85 per cent of high schools charge activity and athletic fees.[45] The activity fees range from $10 to $300 ($44 on average) and athletic fees vary from $1 to $1500 (the average fee is $116). These pay-to-play fees can be a barrier to participating in school activities, especially for children in low income families. In the 2016 C.S. Mott Children's Hospital National Poll on Children's Health a national sample of US parents reported that the cost of participating in sports, clubs, and arts activities in middle and high school resulted in a drop in their children's participation.[46] The drop was higher for children from families earning less than $60,000 per year (27 per cent drop) than for kids from families with an income of more than $60,000 annually (12 per cent drop). Multiple polls conducted by the C.S. Mott Children's Hospital since 2012 show that children from lower income families have lower rates of participation in school activities than their peers from higher income families.

Newfoundland and Labrador's Community Services Council drew similar conclusions in their 2003 study of the impact of school fees and fundraising on social inclusion in the Avalon East School District.[47] Administrators, teachers, parents, and students reported they knew of situations in which children missed out on activities at school due to the cost. Parents and students said children were sometimes kept home or older children skipped school on days when fee-based activities were taking place. Almost half of teachers and administrators reported that attendance dropped on special event days that involved a cost. Twenty-three per cent of students, teachers, and administrators stated they know of at least one situation in which limited financial resources caused a child to be excluded from school activities. More than half of parents surveyed said paying fees was a financial hardship. The study also found that the vast majority of teachers (92 per cent) subsidized students who could not afford field trips, supplies, or other expenses.

A second type of school fee includes those charged to students taking particular courses who want to use better materials or to go on trips related to the course. Lord Byng lists these fees in a second fee schedule, the Standard Supplemental Fee Schedule.[48]

The optional fees are associated with particular courses, including better ingredients for food and nutrition courses, enhanced supplies for arts courses, Advanced Placement exams, and workbook deposits.

The Standard General Fee Schedule also lists fees associated with Lord Byng Arts, a specialized program of choice in the board. A program or school of choice is one that a student opts to attend due to some unique feature, such as a focus on the arts or sports. This is a third type of school fee: it covers the costs associated with attending – or applying to – a school of choice. The cost of the arts program at Lord Byng is $105, quite modest compared to some other specialty schools in the country.[49] Fees associated with the Delta School District's Golf Academy, for example, are more than $3,000 per year, not including golf-club memberships fees.[50]

Specialized programs or schools may also have hidden costs, including transportation expenses and costs related to even qualifying for the program. For example, an elite athletic program in the TDSB requires that program applicants be competing at the provincial level in a sport. To compete at this level normally involves years of significant financial resources and investment in training, travel, equipment, team, and coach fees. Indeed, specialized schools and programs are known to serve students from higher income families and contribute to polarization by class between schools. The TDSB's Enhancing Equity Task Force, a body charged with identifying ways to enhance equity in the board, noted that "specialized schools and programs, along with optional attendance, while benefitting certain populations, have inadvertently resulted in greater competition and disparities between schools."[51] In a draft report the task force recommended phasing these programs out. When some parents of students in TDSB special schools and programs got wind of this draft recommendation, their opposition was fast and furious. Just a few days after the draft report was released, the TDSB's director assured parents that the schools and programs would not be eliminated. Instead, he promised the board would look for ways to improve access for all students.

The False Promise of Fee Waivers

Lord Byng's Fee Schedules refer to a financial hardship policy that states,

> The Board of Education Trustees is committed to ensuring that no school-age student will be denied an opportunity to participate in a course, class or program because of an inability to pay fees. Parents and guardians unable to pay some or all of school a fee [sic] or deposit are invited to speak to their child's teacher, grade counsellor, and/or an administrator.[52]

Policies to reduce or waive fees can be found across the country, although they are not always posted as prominently as they are in Lord Byng's notices.

In Manitoba, for example, schools cannot charge allowable fees "unless the board has established policies and procedures to facilitate participation by students who would otherwise be excluded due to financial hardship."[53] Similarly, New Brunswick's *Contribution of Resources by Parents* policy states, "A student will not be denied full participation in an educational program or co-curricular activity due to an inability to contribute financially."[54]

These policy statements suggest that students whose families can't afford to pay fees won't be excluded from the programs, but this promise may be far from reality. First, the policies assume parents know how to request that fees be waived. This assumption may be mistaken. A survey of teachers by the British Columbia Teachers' Federation (BCTF) in 2012 found that only two-thirds of respondents knew of a process for students, parents, or teachers (on behalf of a student) to apply for financial assistance to cover the costs of school-related materials or activities.[55] Eleven per cent said there was no process to do so at their school. Of the teachers who reported they know the process at their school, 39 per cent said they think parents are "somewhat aware," while just over a quarter said they believe parents are "not very aware" or "not all aware" of what to do. This finding is slightly higher than that of a poll of parents by the C.S. Mott Children's Hospital National Poll on Children's

Health based at the University of Michigan: it found that 19 per cent didn't know about waiver policies.[56] Teachers in the BCTF survey perceived the lowest level of awareness of a process to request financial assistance to be in low income and mixed income schools.

Even if families *do* know about fee waivers, they normally need to reveal their financial hardship when requesting help. Take the waiver process at the Calgary Board of Education (CBE), for example. The board's website states,

> No child is ever denied access to an education in the CBE because of an inability to pay. The CBE has a waiver process for families who can't afford to pay the fees. Visit our Waivers page for more information and the documents required as proof of income.[57]

If parents can't provide documents to prove they can't afford the fees, they can declare "financial hardship" to their school principals, who will help workout a payment plan or waive some or all of the fees.[58] The expectation that parents or students reveal their financial situation to school staff ignores, or worse, dismisses, the stigma people living in poverty experience. More than half the teachers surveyed in 2012 by BCTF believe that parents' or students' discomfort in asking for financial support is a barrier to receiving it. Consequently, school fees exclude some children from activities and resources that their more financially well-off peers enjoy at school. As I mentioned above, almost a quarter of administrators, teachers, parents, and students in a Newfoundland and Labrador study reported they knew of situations in which a child missed out on an activity due to lack of financial resources.

Waiver policies for families that can't afford fees help to normalize the practice of charging fees in public schools by implying that those who can afford to pay should do so. I have yet to come across a waiver policy that recognizes parents who object to paying fees on principle. Instead, the idea is that parents who can afford to pay certain fees should do so. As Michelle Milani and I have argued elsewhere, a fee-for-service approach in schools is based an idea common in the private sector: if you want more, you have to pay more.[59] Like other means of fundraising, allowing schools to charge fees for "extras" enables provincial and territorial governments to claim they are meeting their obligation to provide free education and providing equal opportunities for all students. In so doing, they help legitimate Canada's myth of meritocracy, since, as scholar Rajani Naidoo explains, the perception of an equal playing field is necessary to justify competition and unequal outcomes.[60]

Alternatively, some parents may pay fees they can't afford and suffer the consequences. A parent participant in a community conversation conducted by York Region District School Board's Classism/Poverty Sub-Committee in 2018 explained the dilemma:

> This year I will have 3 children in high school ... school fees, gym uniforms, club membership fees, sports team fees ... If I cannot afford it; my kids will lose out on playing on sports teams or joining clubs which will enrich their lives.[61]

In its 2019 survey of school principals People for Education found that on average only 3 per cent of students request to have fees waived, even though Statistics Canada reports that 14 per cent of people in Ontario live below the poverty line. This finding suggests that parents who can't afford fees don't know about waivers, don't ask for fees to be waived, or pay them anyway.

Resisting School Fees

There is resistance to school fees, however. In 2016, Quebec mother Daisye Marcil launched a class action lawsuit against sixty-eight school boards in the province who allowed schools to charge fees.[62] The case argued that the fees violated Quebec's Education Act, which guarantees a free education to resident elementary and secondary school-age children. The government directed boards to determine what schools provide and what parents should contribute by December 2017. In turn, boards in Montreal asked the government clarify the meaning of a "free education." The lawsuit was settled out of court in July 2018, and while admitting no guilt, the boards agreed to pay parents who paid fees between the 2009–10 (or 2010–11, depending on the board) and 2016–17 school years up to $24.09 per student per year.[63] Boards paid a total of $153,507,134.

In 2018, the Quebec government held public consultations on the issue of fees. The findings show that many respondents are in favour of parents paying something towards their children's education in public schools. Specifically, 66.2 per cent of participants supported some fees for school activities and trips; 49 per cent supported some fees for school supplies; and 67.3 per cent supported some fees for specific projects or programs.[64] Quebec legislators passed new laws in 2019 in an effort to clarify what is and is not part of its "free education." According to a document (i.e., *Memory Aid*) on the government's website,[65] free education includes free textbooks, instructional materials, and educational services for every preschool, elementary, and secondary school student in a Quebec public school. Many aspects of vocational training and adult general education for students under eighteen (or twenty-one if the student is disabled) are also included. Free education does *not* include school supplies, notebooks, locks, special materials, specialized programs, and more.

In 2019, Alberta's government introduced Alberta Regulation 95/2019. It prohibits school boards from charging fees for textbooks, workbooks, printing, photocopying, and paper. School boards must post school fees in a fee schedule, consult with parents before setting, raising, or reducing fees, and demonstrate the need for the fees. They also have to show that fees have been spent to cover intended costs as well as create a process for parents to request a fee waiver.

Charging fees, then, is a policy that undermines the public school ideal. This practice generally limits access to opportunities considered enrichment or enhancements to the regular school program to students whose families can afford to pay for them. Waiver policies designed to mitigate this situation rely on families knowing they exist and exposing their financial situation to school staff, ignoring the stigma attached to people with low incomes. Furthermore, kids from families most likely to afford the fees are also more likely to have access to advantages outside of school. Pay-to-play policies, like fundraising, exacerbate existing inequalities and are inequitable. And denying kids their timetables is just wrong – not to mention illegal.

I understand why schools charge fees. Parents and students want specialized programs and extracurricular opportunities that cater to kids' interests. No doubt these benefit participants; but such benefits should be available to all students in a public school. Allowing parents to pay fees to get more for their own children than the basic education program provides constructs public education as a commodity and tips the balance towards prioritizing individual interests over the public good. In the next section I examine how Canadian school districts engage in a fundraising practice that reproduces these outcomes on a global scale.

International Student Recruitment

Up to this point I've focused on how individual schools raise funds to supplement public funding. I turn now to a strategy many school districts use to raise money: hosting tuition-paying international students. This strategy is just one among many. Other approaches include renting school facilities, selling advertising space, and offering continuing education courses to adult learners. Like schools, governments permit districts to fundraise. BC's government went even further in 2002, however, when it gave its districts greater responsibility for generating funds, purportedly to enable them to better meet their local needs, as part of a number of reforms that established school markets in the province's public education system. Funds could come from the private or public sectors. University of British Columbia researchers Wendy Poole and Gerald Fallon explain: "Whereas, previously, government was the exclusive provider of funding, now they became an enabler responsible for providing opportunities to school districts to compete for both public [via enrolment-focused funding] and private funds."[66] This shift in the government's role from funder to education-market enabler exemplifies a new role for states under neoliberalism. Between 2002 and 2012, BC districts increased their revenue from private sources by 22 per cent.

Researchers, policymakers, and the media have paid a lot of attention to international students in universities and colleges across Canada and far less to those studying in elementary and high schools. In 2019, the Canadian Bureau for International Education, a Canadian organization dedicated exclusively to supporting international education from K–12 to postgraduate studies, reported there were 52,135 international students studying in Canada's public and private secondary and elementary schools.[67] Students may come for a few weeks, the summer, a year, or longer. And their numbers are growing. In BC, for example, the number of K–12 international students went from 12,000 in 2012 to more than 20,000 in 2017,[68] and the number of international students studying in Ontario's TDSB increased nearly 58 per cent between 2014–15 and 2018–19.[69] The countries that send the most K–12 students to Canada include China, South Korea, Brazil, Japan, India, and Vietnam.[70]

Since international students do not meet residency requirements that entitle them to receive education for free, they pay tuition, normally directly to districts. Tuition can cost upwards of $15,000 annually (plus accommodation, food, and out-of-school expenses such as phone, Internet, shopping, entertainment, and other expenses). This makes international students a lucrative source of funding for boards. With the growth in international student numbers has come greater revenues for receiving boards. The number of international students attending schools in the TCDSB, for example, increased almost tenfold between 2010–11 and 2015–16; consequently, revenue from fees increased to more than eleven times the amount generated in 2010–11.[71] Although as we shall see, not all boards and schools benefit equally from the increased funding that comes with international student tuition.

Hosting international students is just one facet of international education; there are many associated ideas and practices across Canada. Canadian students may study abroad as part of student exchange programs, and some educators go overseas to teach. Domestic curriculum may introduce Canadian students to international perspectives and cultures, and some schools offer courses in languages other than English and French. Many of these practices have been around for decades, offer engaging learning experiences, and help achieve important educational goals. Even hosting fee-paying international students is not new. As the figures above indicate, however, the number of these students studying in Canada has increased substantially in recent years as part of what is now the international education marketplace. Countries around the world are competing for students who are seeking international education experiences.

Benefits and Costs of International Education

Some provinces have formal international education strategies designed to increase the number of international students studying in the province or formal programs. Manitoba even has legislation and regulations that govern international education in the province. Support for hosting international students in other provinces can be found on government websites.

Governments cite social, cultural, and especially economic benefits of international education. Alberta's International Strategy 2013, for example, explains that

> students, parents, schools and communities gain a broader understanding of the world and Alberta's place in it when interacting with people with multiple perspectives. Engaging in international education also contributes to diversifying Alberta's economy – as international students pay tuition fees and other expenditures related to living in Alberta communities.[72]

Similarly, BC's Ministry of Education and Training explains on its "International Education Information for Administrators" webpage,

> International Education in British Columbia (B.C.) supports diversity and inclusion, and enables the development of intercultural competencies for B.C. students, teachers and communities. The expansion of international education helps to create new relationships between British Columbia and other regions and cultures around the world. It is also an important economic driver as the third largest export sector for the province … [73]

Ontario's then-minister of education, Liz Sandals, introduced the province's International Education Strategy in 2015 by stating,

> Ontario's Strategy for K–12 International Education will expand and enrich the learning environment for all students and educators, providing opportunities to embrace diversity and achieve excellence through learning about and from other cultures and education systems.
>
> The benefits of this strategy extend beyond the classroom and into our communities, building social, cultural, and economic opportunities now and for the future. Students studying in Ontario contribute over $4 billion to our economy each year, and generate over 30,000 jobs.[74]

As these three quotes make clear, international education is valued by governments for much more than its benefits for international and domestic students. Despite their assertions that international education supports diversity and enriches learning about other cultures (which it might), I've yet to find a government scholarship generous enough to enable young people from a wide range of countries and social classes to attend Canadian elementary or secondary schools. Instead, international education is promoted primarily as a way to boost economies and create jobs.

International education does indeed impact the economy. A 2016 Alberta Education report states that the annual economic impact of the province's 2,444 fee-paying K–12 international students and their visiting friends and relatives is $66.4 million.[75] Further, they support 670 jobs. In BC, the direct and indirect impact of international student spending in 2017 totaled $386.4 million dollars.[76] These benefits come at significant cost to the public education ideal, however.

First, turning to tuition-paying students for funds to supplement government funding undermines the idea that public schools should be fully funded by the government. While BC's policy may be the most explicit, all provinces encourage their boards to consider international student recruitment as a means to top up funding. Tuition dollars may enable schools to fill classrooms and offer resources and opportunities they otherwise could not due to declining enrolment and limited government funding. This funding is not secure, however. The manager of Vancouver School Board's International Education Program explained the precarity of the situation to researcher Johanna Waters: "The fact is if there was an economic crash in Korea tomorrow it would devastate every single international programme in Canada ... So it is driven by factors completely out of our control."[77] Like other forms of fundraising, looking to the private sector to fill funding shortfalls lets governments off the hook to provide adequate funds for public education.

Second, researchers Wendy Poole, Gerald Fallon, and Vicheth Sen show that boards are not equally able to attract international students and their funds due to districts' geographic location and associated social factors.[78] Their study of international student funding in BC's school districts found that urban districts typically generate more tuition funds than rural districts. More specifically, the four lowest tuition-generating districts in their study, all rural boards, did not generate any tuition at all, while the highest four added between 8.7 per cent and 18.8 per cent to the base amounts they receive per student from the government. This means that some districts have much more money to spend on programs and resources for their students than others. Thus, policies and efforts to attract international students can create inequities between boards.

Furthermore, since not all districts or provinces can compete for international students only Canadian students, staff, and communities in the "winning boards" have opportunities to enjoy the social and cultural benefits of living and working alongside international students. And there *are* benefits for students. A 2016 study for Alberta's Ministry of Education found that 82 per cent of participants from school authorities reported that the presence of K–12 international students increase local students' tolerance towards other cultures and ethnicities. A majority of them also said the presence of international students positively impacted Canadian students' personal development and as well as the local community.[79]

Inequities can also arise between boards that *do* attract international students. Ryan Deschambault, a researcher examining the relationship between English as an additional language education and international education in BC's public education system, explains that boards that serve English language learners (ELLs) can add international students to existing English as second language (ESL) classes and use tuition funds elsewhere since the BC government provides funds for domestic ELLs.[80] Boards that otherwise would not serve ELLs and therefore do not have government funding to provide ESL classes must use international students' tuition to offer them when needed.

When boards and compete with each other for international students, their staff have to change how they work and think more like their counterparts in the private sector. People may be hired or reassigned to develop marketing strategies and recruit students. A school administrator in a study by researchers Merli Tamtik and Angela O'Brien-Klewchuk reported, "I think it's the marketing strategies that have brought success ... we will go on recruitment trips to Germany and to South America, to Spain, Italy, because we want to grow those markets."[81] Recruitment activities and positions dedicated to international education may take resources away from domestic students and local educational issues. Boards may be encouraged to think of other boards as "the competition" and to prioritize their own constituents' needs over those of students, families, and staff in other boards. As a consequence, the "public interest" served by boards in the education market will become smaller and limited to people associated with a particular school board.

The ideal of public schools serving the public interest gets further diminished when you consider the findings of Tamtik and O'Brien-Klewchuk's investigation of the reasons international students and their parents chose Manitoba, Canada, as a place to study. The main reason cited by both students and parents is to boost students' career prospects in the global marketplace.[82] Learning English and possibly French are viewed as key skills for success. They also cite the potential to learn about other cultures and developing a global perspective, as they believe these could be useful if students choose to immigrate someplace else.

International students and their parents also choose schooling in Canada to improve students' chances of getting into their preferred university. Many selected Canada in particular because Canadian schools have a better reputation for providing high quality education compared to the other English-speaking countries they considered. Tamtik and O'Brien-Klewchuk's findings highlight the private interests pursued by international students and their families in public schools in Manitoba. The idea of contributing to the interests of Canadians is totally absent. What comes across instead is a concept of public education as a commodity that offers private benefits to those who buy it – the antithesis to the idea of a public education that prioritizes the public good.

Of course, this commodity is not available to every family outside Canada – only those who can afford it. The cost of attending school in Canada can easily run more than $20,000 a year. Johanna Waters details how upper-middle-class families in Hong Kong seek international education opportunities for their children in Canada as a way to avoid competition for academic opportunities at home and to acquire highly valued academic credentials and cultural capital.[83] Upon their return, these students are more likely to obtain employment than their locally educated peers. Thus, not only does the local credential become devalued but students reproduce their own class advantage. Canadian school boards' commodification of public education, then, facilitates inequality on a global scale as well as within Canada's own borders.

When schools and districts turn to private funding to cover their expenses, they move further away from the public school ideal. Rather than being places where all children have the same opportunity to access free education and reap its benefits, they become sites where the already advantaged acquire more privileges and secure their position. Administrators and teachers must shift energy away from teaching, learning, and advocating for all students and towards meeting demands of funders and consumers in the education marketplace. While the grandparent who shops at the school book fair, the parent who applies for a grant to support the music program, the teacher who asks for five dollars for a field trip, and the district administrator who helps an international student find a place to stay may be doing what they believe to be good for *their* kids and students, governments are allowed to divest in public education that benefits all Canada's children.

chapter four

Securing Private Benefits

Tracey and her husband, Mike, confronted their first school choice when their daughter, Charlotte, was in JK. Should they enrol her in French Immersion for SK or keep her in the English program? Tracey understood the benefits and drawbacks of learning in French: she'd been in an Extended French program in high school. Since acceptance to French Immersion at Charlotte's school was determined by lottery, Tracey decided to put Charlotte's name in and let fate decide. Tracey thought, "If she gets in she gets in, and if she doesn't she doesn't." At first, Charlotte didn't secure a spot, but later a place opened up, and they decided they'd take it.

At the start of grade 6, the parents of Charlotte's friends began talking about school options for the next year. While all the kids had confirmed places in a local middle school's French Immersion program, the school had a reputation for being a bit "tough." While not exactly sure what this meant, Tracey thought it had something to do with the kids that come from a poorer neighbourhood in the catchment area. There was also a rumour that a student's dad was beat up by some kids in grade 8. In any case, Tracey wasn't sure that Charlotte should continue in French Immersion. While Charlotte was fine with French Immersion, she didn't love it like some of her friends did. Tracey didn't want to force her to stay in the program if there were other things that interested her more. In particular, Charlotte liked math and science, and Tracey wondered if Charlotte would get more out of learning these subjects in English, her first language. Plus, thinking ahead a few years, Tracey worried about Charlotte having to travel by public transit to the nearest high school with a French Immersion program. And although Charlotte hadn't articulated it, Tracey could sense she wasn't thrilled about going to the local middle school. She wasn't interested in boys, social media, make-up, and the latest teen fashions. "What are Charlotte's options?" she began to wonder.

Throughout the fall term, Charlotte's school sent home details about upcoming open houses for various middle schools and specialized programs. This was all new to Tracey. Where she grew up, most kids went to their local schools. Some, like her, went to Extended French or French Immersion programs, and some went into gifted programs. These were the only options she knew about. Her parents certainly hadn't gone to any open houses for middle or high school. At first she thought the whole thing was ridiculous, but she started to wonder if she was being dismissive, to Charlotte's detriment. So Tracey talked to other parents in Charlotte's class and did some research online about various schools. She learned about an alternative school in her neighbourhood called New Heights. It was actually closer to her home than the middle school with French Immersion, and location was an important consideration for Tracey. While the school had been there for decades, Tracey hadn't heard of it. She was intrigued by the description of the school's teaching approach on its website and decided to check it out.

Parents lined up around the block on the day of New Heights' open house. Students gave tours of the school, located on the top floor of a regular K–6 public school. It has just one grade 7 class and one grade 8 class, each with thirty-six kids. While teachers follow the provincial curriculum, they deliver it differently from most schools. Instead of spreading all subjects out across the year, kids study different subject areas in depth for concentrated periods of time. They might do three weeks of intense math, for example, and then the next few weeks do something else. New Heights also emphasizes outdoor learning, spending lots of time in the park across the street. The kids even go on three overnight trips each year (paid for by parents and other fundraising). What's more, according to people Tracey spoke with, the school focuses on math and science. These aspects of the school appealed to Tracey, Mike, and Charlotte.

So, too, did the size of the school. Tracey thought Charlotte would feel less intimidated about the transition to grade 7 in a smaller school. Plus, Tracey and Mike got the feeling that students at New Heights were able to be "kids" for just a bit longer than seemed to be the case in their local middle school. She thought this appealed to Charlotte, although Charlotte didn't say so. Tracey talked to parents of current students as well as graduates from decades past who spoke glowingly about their experiences in alternative schools. Charlotte's grade 6 teacher pointed out that if Charlotte went to New Heights and didn't like it she could go to the local middle school and probably even get back into French Immersion. That is, she'd still have options. Tracey also liked the fact that if Charlotte went to New Heights the question about whether she'd travel to a French Immersion program for high school out of the neighbourhood would be settled. Not only would Charlotte not have to travel far, but also Tracey thought her daughter would probably be better off taking university prerequisites in English. They decided to apply.

As was the case for French Immersion in SK, luck would play a role in determining if Charlotte would actually get a spot at New Heights. Potential students complete an application for admission, and their names are placed in a lottery. Some of the spaces are set aside for students from traditionally marginalized groups. After some discussion, Tracey decided to indicate that Charlotte is racialized. While Charlotte passes as white, her paternal grandparents were both Asian Canadian.

The draw took place on Valentine's Day. The whole family gathered anxiously around the computer as New Heights posted the names of lucky students as they were drawn. Tracey, Mike, and Charlotte all shrieked with excitement when Charlotte's name appeared on the screen. They literally felt like they had won the lottery.

In the last chapter I showed how schools' and districts' efforts to generate funds from private sources help position public education as primarily a private rather than a public good. This chapter also focuses on policies and parent practices that position it that way but without the emphasis on raising money. Instead, I focus on the ways education policies and private resources interact to enable some kids, usually those from advantaged backgrounds, to accumulate more private benefits from public education systems than many of their peers. As I explained in chapter 1, what constitutes a "public system" varies across the country. Thus, not all the policies I discuss in the chapter exist in each province.

I begin by discussing various K–12 schooling options across Canada typically introduced with promises to better meet students' interests and parents' preferences by offering more choice in education. While theoretically available to all children, I show that most school choice policies disproportionately benefit white and affluent kids by providing them access to special learning opportunities. I then turn to ways parents use their money to pay for services outside of school that give their children advantages inside them. Specifically, I talk about parents paying for private psychological testing, purchasing individual course credits from private schools, sending their kids to private tutoring services, and creating "learning pods" during the COVID-19 pandemic. Again, in theory, these options are available to every parent, but in reality only those with money can access them. In each discussion I attempt to review Canadian research that shows the outcomes of these policies and practices for Black, racialized, and Indigenous children, but this information is sorely lacking. We know a lot more about how school choice policies impact kids differently by class than by other markers of identity. As you read, keep in mind that racialized and Indigenous children in Canada are more likely to be poor than their non-racialized and non-Indigenous peers.

Education Markets

In chapter 1, I discussed endogenous privatization: the introduction of ideas, practices, and values of the private sector into public education. Some of the clearest examples of this form of privatization in Canada are policies that organize education systems as markets. In these arrangements parents and their children (the markets' consumers) choose between different schools or school programs based on their preferences and resources. Schools are funded based on enrolment: the more students who attend a school, the more money the schools receive. American scholar Chris Lubienski explains that a consumer model privatizes the purpose of a public good such as education by reconfiguring it as a commodity; that is, as something to be selected by individuals who act in their own self-interest.[1] The story of Tracey's experience choosing an alternative school for her daughter, Charlotte, illustrates an education market operating at the district level, while in the last chapter I explained how customers (families) outside our borders purchase Canadian public education as part of a global education marketplace. By sending their kids to Canada for schooling, these parents are hedging their bets that their children will have a better chance of entering desired universities, securing future employment, and enhancing their standing in their home countries.

Supporters of expanding markets in education argue that schools' need to compete for students will force them to improve and customize their offerings and enhance the overall quality of schools. Many claim that teachers and other workers in public education systems are doing a poor job and have little incentive to change or improve their practices. As evidence they point to stagnant academic outcomes despite increased education spending or long-standing poor outcomes for various groups, particularly the most marginalized in society. In the United States, supporters of new forms of schooling and school choice include conservatives who view public schools as inefficient, as well as some (although certainly not all) communities of colour fed up with the continued inability and maybe even unwillingness of traditional public schools to meet their children's needs.[2] In Canada, institutional advocates of school choice policies include the Fraser Institute, the C.D. Howe Institute, and the Atlantic Institute for Market Studies (AIMS; part of the Fraser Institute as of November 2019). These supporters argue that parental and student support for school choice is evident in their demand for and uptake of opportunities to select specialized schools and programs.

Indeed, many Canadian parents do participate in some form of school choice. Although options vary across the country, all provinces have more than one kind of schooling available. Drawing on data from a national survey of parents in Canada in 2005, Canadian researchers Scott Davies and Janice Aurini examined whether and how parents choose between secular public, religious public, and private schools. One of their key findings is that nearly two-thirds of parents participate in some form of choosing between schools.[3] While one-third does so by selecting a school *other than* their local public school, the other third choose their local school when deciding where to live. While you might expect this to be the case for parents who have high enough incomes to buy homes wherever they'd like, Aurini and Davies didn't find any difference between parents with high or low incomes. However, they did find that family finances and parents' education increase the likelihood that parents will engage in school choice.

In a 2017 study that examined how racialized and Indigenous parents with low incomes choose schools in Vancouver, researchers Ee-Seul Yoon and Chris Lubienski found, like Aurini and Davies, that a third chose elementary schools other than their assigned ones.[4] However these families' elementary school choices were strongly impacted by where they lived. Housing decisions came before school choices. Even if they would have liked to have lived elsewhere, their options were limited by the availability of affordable housing. For the families who were able to choose schools, they were able to do so only because the family owned a car or the schools were close to home or offered free transportation.

School choice policies are based on the belief that parents are rational actors who make decisions based on careful cost-benefit analyses. They might consult different kinds of information to help them choose, including standardized test scores and graduation rates. In fact, school choice policies have encouraged policies and practices that generate this information about public schools. Schools and programs of choice may also require kids to complete applications, write exams, sit for interviews, audition, and pay fees. Securing a spot often demands knowledge of deadlines, program expectations, transportation, and money. And not all parents have the same access to these resources.

Yoon and Lubienski's study also shows that choosing schools is more than a rational decision. The parents interviewed said how they think their children will feel and fit in at the school matters too. In particular, parents with low incomes said they wouldn't feel comfortable sending their kids to private schools or schools in affluent neighbourhoods even if they could afford them. Instead, they preferred to send their kids to schools with children in a similar income bracket. Indigenous families in the study said that choosing schools in neighbourhoods where there were other Indigenous children was important as well. They worried about their children being bullied or excluded if they were the only Indigenous ones.[5] Yoon and Lubienski's findings align with conclusions drawn by researchers examining school choosers outside Canada too: not all families are equally likely – or have the same ability – to participate in school choice.[6] They also reflect research that demonstrates a school's demographics may be more important to parents than its students' academic performance.[7] That is, parents tend to choose schools attended by kids like their own.

So how do school choice policies enable parents to secure advantages for their own children? A first step is choosing a school or school program as described in the narrative that opened this chapter. Many policies introduced at the district and provincial levels in the past few decades have increased the variety of schools that exist and make it easier for kids to attend schools outside their local neighbourhoods. In this section I review various school programs and types in Canada's education marketplaces, beginning with options offered within public systems, then moving to charter schools, private schools, and finally, homeschooling. Not all provinces offer the same choices, and options go by different names in different places. Notably, I don't discuss religious schools as a discrete school type because in some provinces Catholic schools fall into the category of public schools, whereas in other places all faith-based options are found strictly in private schools. I show that while some choice policies may be introduced in the name of making it easier for kids to attend schools that best meet their needs and interests, the students who benefit most are often those from advantaged (i.e., typically white and middle or high income) families.

Open Enrolment

Historically, a family's ability to choose a school was often limited to moving to a particular neighbourhood since many districts assign kids their schools based on where they live. As I mentioned above, deciding where to live remains an important form of school choice for a third of Canadian parents. This figure explains why efforts to redraw the boundaries of a school's catchment area can become a battle between districts and parents.[8] While many districts still follow this practice, they may also have open enrolment policies that allow kids to attend schools *outside* their catchment area but *within* their school district. Quebec actually mandates that districts allow these intradistrict school transfers. A few governments (BC, Alberta, and Manitoba) require open enrolment *between* districts across the province, although some restrictions may apply. A school might deny out-of-catchment students if it doesn't have space for them, for example. Allowing open enrolment within or across school district boundaries facilitates school choice and education markets because parents and students can choose public schools outside their neighbourhoods.

Open boundary policies are supposed to enable parents to choose schools they feel are best suited for their children. Research in the United States shows that when choosing a school other than their local school, families tend to choose schools that have higher student achievement and lower percentages of students from low income backgrounds, minority students, students with limited English-language proficiency, and students in special education programs.[9] Choosing schools does not necessarily result in higher student achievement for students, however. A study of the academic outcomes of open enrolment in Los Angeles found there were no differences in achievement test scores for white, multiethnic, or Black students. However, Asian and Latino students' scores were higher in their chosen schools. Disparities in achievement between students of different races remained in both chosen and local schools.[10]

Importantly, researchers have found that not all families are equally able or likely to take advantage of open enrolment. Based on their analyses of five years of student enrolment data in Colorado's public schools, researchers Lesley Lavery and Deven Carlson found that when it comes to interdistrict enrolment, affluent students are more likely to choose schools outside their district than their socioeconomically disadvantaged peers.[11] They also found that students who are English language learners or who have disabilities are less likely to enrol in schools outside their districts than their English-speaking and non-disabled peers. These findings echo those of Yoon and Lubienski's study of within-district school choosing described above. Many parents in their study were unable to take advantage of the open enrolment policy unless schools were close to home. When it came to choosing secondary schools, families with lower incomes were less likely to participate than families in higher income brackets even though older kids would likely be able to travel alone. When they did participate, their kids attended schools closer to their homes than other children. Notably, the Vancouver School Board, like many boards, does not provide transportation or transit subsidies to kids who choose schools other than their assigned local schools. Families must cover the costs.

The findings of these studies suggest that advantaged families can more easily use open enrolment policies to choose schools than can disadvantaged families. Further, research in the United States shows that while all families choose schools with better academic records than their local schools, advantaged parents choose the most affluent schools with the highest records, while disadvantaged families choose schools that have lower rates of poverty and only slightly stronger academic records than their assigned ones.[12] Parents also tend to choose schools attended by children like their own. Thus, in some cases, particularly in racially, ethnically, and economically diverse areas, schools – both chosen schools and schools left behind – become more socially stratified.[13]

These outcomes are a problem for the public school ideal. A key concern is that kids in high-poverty, racially segregated schools do not have the same access to opportunities and benefits of public schooling as kids in diverse schools. In their recent report, *How Racially Diverse Schools and Classrooms Can Benefit All Students*, Amy Stuart Wells, Lauren Fox, and Diana Cordova-Cobo summarize research on the impacts of attending racially and socioeconomically diverse schools for students. Their review finds that there is a negative relationship between students' academic achievement and attending a high-poverty, racially segregated school.[14] In more racially diverse schools, however, Black and Hispanic kids' achievement improved, while white students' achievement remained the same. Part of the explanation, the authors reason, is due to students' equitable access to resources that support learning. Teachers and students in diverse schools also hold higher expectations for students than those in racially segregated schools. Further, learning alongside peers with different backgrounds and perspectives promotes creativity, deeper learning, motivation, and the development of problem-solving abilities and critical-thinking skills for all students, including white middle-class kids. It also helps students reflect critically on their own ideas and promotes tolerance of different viewpoints. The benefits of diverse schools, then, are shared by all students. Thus, policies that exclude students, even if not their intent, stand in the way of achieving the public school ideal.

Alternative and Specialized Schools and Programs

When parents choose schools under open enrolment policies, they often do it so their children can attend a program not available in their local school. Lord Byng Arts, the school I discussed in the last chapter, is an example of a specialized school in the Vancouver School Board. Specialized programs or schools, "projets particuliers" in Quebec, offer something in addition to the regular school program. The "something" might be a particular curriculum focus (e.g., arts, science, athletics, foreign language, leadership, culture), an accelerated pace of learning, an academic program, such as the International Baccalaureate or Advanced Placement courses, or alternative pedagogical approach (e.g., Montessori).

In some places there is an important distinction between alternative schools and specialized schools and programs. Many alternative schools were introduced across the country to offer a more progressive approach to schooling or to better support students who were poorly served in traditional schools, some before the advent of neoliberalism.[15] The TDSB's Afrocentric public school is an example of alternative school created to integrate "the diverse perspectives, experiences and histories of people of African descent into the provincial mandated curriculum."[16] The school was created in 2009 following much advocacy by Toronto's Black communities, who demonstrated that Black students were underserved in the TDSB's public schools.[17] Researchers Philip Howard and Carl James report that the school provides a sense of community for Black students, teachers, and parents.[18] Teachers strive to affirm Black students' identities and address challenges with students and parents in ways different from the anti-Black approaches typically adopted in other schools. A review of the school found that its students' achievement on Ontario's standardized tests for grades 3 and 6 was improving at a higher rate than other schools in similar circumstances.[19]

Alternative schools and programs designed to address systemic inequalities of public schooling are unusual. Policies that enabled the creation of these programs have, in some cases, since been used to create new schooling options as part of expanding education markets.[20] In other places policies have been created expressly for that purpose. Often, specialized schools are used to attract high-achieving students.[21] Research on the effects of specialized programs on student achievement are mixed. Much of what we know about specialized programs comes from studies of magnet programs in the United States. Like specialized programs, magnet programs offer courses or instructional approaches that differ from those offered by regular public schools. They were originally introduced as part of desegregation efforts. Based on an analysis of eighteen studies of magnet schools' effects on student outcomes, researchers Jia Wang, Joan Herman, and Daniel Dockterman concluded that while their effects on student achievement overall are minimal or modest, they are more effective than traditional public schools for students at risk and for below-average readers.[22] Scholar Julie Harris, on the other hand, found zero or negative effects on students' reading and math achievement scores in programs that focused on the performing arts, humanities, or college preparation.[23] As I will show below, however, specialized schools and programs often perpetuate social inequality.

In the Vancouver District School Board, specialized programs are known as mini schools. Mini schools "provide enrichment opportunities for highly motivated students who are Vancouver residents and consistently work at an Applying level and have excellent work habits."[24] Specialized programs and mini schools are usually located inside regular public high schools, with students from the two programs sharing facilities. Students may also take some classes together. Sometimes an entire school may have a special focus, such as Lord Byng Arts. Parents and students perceive specialized arts schools and programs as offering a better educational experience than regular public high schools.[25]

The TDSB offers a number of specialized programs as well. Some are work-focused programs, such the Ontario Youth Apprenticeship Program (OYAP) and Specialist High Skills Major Program (SHSMP), or dual-credit programs where students earn college and high school credits. Others offer alternative schedules or teaching approaches, such as one-to-one instruction or independent learning. There are also interest-driven programs, including elite athlete and arts-focused programs, as well as ones with a heavy academic focus, including the International Baccalaureate (IB) and Advanced Placement programs (AP). The work-focused and alternate programs are not geared towards the same groups of students as the specialized programs and schools, nor are they as socially valued. Table 2 shows student enrolment in IB, AP, elite athlete, OYAP, and SHSMP by racial category in 2011–12. The figures are based on data collected through the board's student survey.

It's plain to see from Table 2 that the secondary school specialized programs' enrolment patterns do not reflect those of the TDSB overall. Black and Latin American students are overrepresented in OYAP and SHSMP, the work-focused programs, and underrepresented in IB, AP, and elite athletic programs. In the TDSB, work-focused programs are located primarily in Toronto's lowest income neighbourhoods.[26] While white students don't appear to be overrepresented in any specialty programs other than athletic ones and OYAP, this can be explained in part by their disproportionally high enrolment in French Immersion (55.4 per cent; discussed below) and self-contained gifted classes (41.6 per cent).

They may also be in the board's arts-focused programs. Rueben Gaztambide-Fernández and Gillian Parekh's research shows that more than half of the incoming classes at three specialty arts-focused programs come from the highest income brackets in the TDSB. In addition, white students were overrepresented when compared to students in the TDSB's elementary schools, while students from other ethno-racial groups, including South Asian, Black, East Asian, and Other, were significantly underrepresented (students with "mixed" backgrounds are exceptions). Students in

Table 2. Racial Categories across Selected In-school Programs 2011–12 (Excluding Gifted and Special Education)

Self-Identified Race	Aboriginal	Black	East Asian	Latin American	Middle Eastern	Mixed	South Asian	Southeast Asian	White
AP	0.0%	6.0%	37.3%	0.9%	2.6%	4.4%	17.9%	5.9%	25.0%
Elite Athlete	0.0%	7.4%	1.1%	0.4%	1.5%	12.6%	3.0%	1.1%	73.0%
IB	0.0%	5.9%	23.0%	0.5%	4.1%	4.3%	40.8%	4.8%	16.5%
OYAP	0.7%	16.7%	8.6%	2.7%	4.8%	7.7%	18.0%	5.2%	35.6%
SHSMP	0.1%	21.3%	9.1%	4.8%	6.5%	10.3%	21.6%	5.3%	20.9%
Total in TDSB Secondary Schools	0.3%	12.6%	17.9%	2.2%	5.8%	6.9%	21.0%	4.9%	28.3%

Source: Gillian Parekh, "Selected In-School Programs: An Overview (Fact Sheet 8)" (Toronto, ON: Toronto District School Board, 2013), 3.
Notes: AP = Advanced Placement program; IB = International Baccalaureate program; OYAP = Ontario Youth Apprenticeship Program; SHSMP = Specialist High Skills Major Program; TDSB = Toronto District School Board.

the arts-focused program cohort were also more likely to have university-educated parents than the general elementary school population. Gaztambide-Fernández and Parekh demonstrate that while admission processes may favour kids with access to specialized training (i.e., more affluent kids) there is more to the story. They also show that while the programs are open (in theory) to kids from all 195 elementary schools in the board, more than half of them come from just 18 schools and more than a quarter from only 5. Digging deeper, they found that students in schools that send between eleven and twenty kids to the programs are more likely to be affluent and white than schools that send ten or fewer students. They are the students most likely to feel a sense of belonging at school when compared to kids coming from other sending schools as well as kids attending other high schools. Gaztambide-Fernández and Parekh's findings show that enrolment patterns in the arts-focused schools are not simply outcomes of individual choices. Rather, kids who choose these programs make their decisions within a homogenous context marked by economic privilege, whiteness, and high levels of social and cultural capital.

It's not like governments and school boards aren't aware of the effects on equity of specialized programs. In 2016, Quebec's Conseil supérieur de l'éducation released *Steering the Course Back to Equity in Education: Report of the State and Needs of Education 2014–2016.* In it, the conseil stated, "The stratification of the offer in compulsory education – brought about by a proliferation of selective special programs and private schools – is leading to **an unequal treatment that tends to favour the more fortunate**" [emphasis in original].[27] As I discussed in the last chapter, the TDSB's Enhancing Equity Task Force, the body responsible for identifying ways to enhance equity in the board in 2016, came to a similar conclusion about its specialized schools and programs and its optional attendance policy.

The TDSB's data paint a compelling picture of who is enrolled in its specialized schools and programs. Unfortunately, similar data for other boards and their programs across the country are hard to come by. There's no reason to believe patterns in the TDSB are unique to this board, however. In their study of school choice practices by Indigenous families in Vancouver, Ee-Seul Yoon and Lyn Daniels show that the city's Indigenous students are less likely to attend specialized secondary school programs than their non-Indigenous peers. While Indigenous students make up 3 per cent of the board's secondary school population, only 1 per cent of selective programs' students are Indigenous. They are even underrepresented in the specialized program at the high school with the highest proportion of Indigenous kids![28] That is, while 30 per cent of the kids at Britannia Secondary School were Indigenous at the time of the study, only 7 per cent of the students in its specialized programs were Indigenous.

While many specialized programs may have been introduced with the intent to increase student engagement and encourage education innovations, their enrolment patterns are troublesome for the public school ideal. In the last chapter I explained that many specialized programs charge fees – including application fees and fees for special materials or opportunities – that may deter some kids from applying. Some programs' admission criteria also favour financially well-off families, such as the requirement that kids compete at a provincial level at a program for elite athletes, since the expectation can only be met if families can afford to pay for training outside schools. When fees issues are considered along-side findings of Gaztambide-Fernández and Parekh's study and Yoon and Lubienski's research on marginalized parents' school choice practices, it's clear that choices between schools and pro-grams are constrained for some parents by their economic and so-cial contexts. Indigenous families' choices are further constrained by Canada's historical and contemporary settler-colonial practices.

There are other ways that many specialized programs and schools exclude kids who might enjoy and benefit from them. Sometimes it's academic criteria, like at VSB's mini schools. Sometimes it's more. Montreal's Fine Arts Core Education (FACE) elementary and high schools, for example, states that its applicants for 2020–1

> must have a school record indicating no particular difficulties. The re-quirements of the FACE program require rather autonomous students: no failure at the end of the school year in basic subjects at the end of the year.[29]

In addition, "socialization" and "independence" are criteria for high school applicants, in addition to proficiency in the language of instruction (English or French) and an interest in the arts. Finally, "The school welcomes up to 25% of special needs students. The school therefore reserves the right to refuse a child who presents particular difficulties which would require an accompaniment which it cannot offer or if it considers that it cannot adequately meet the needs of a young person."[30] These criteria make it clear that not everyone has the choice to attend FACE. Indeed, many specialized schools and programs have similar exclusion criteria. It's no wonder that Gaztambide-Fernández and Parekh conclude that "choice schemes are not simply an opportunity for individu-als to pursue their idiosyncratic interests and/or talents, but are also a key mechanism through which structural inequalities are reproduced."[31]

French Immersion

One of the most popular choice options across Canada is French Immersion. Parents literally line up for days to enrol their kids in French Immersion programs in some places. These programs offer

English-speaking kids the majority of their instruction in French. Interest in and growth of French Immersion programs followed Canada's Official Languages Act in 1969. French Immersion programs can receive federal funding as part of efforts to support French-language learning.[32] There are at least some public schools in every province and territory that offer French Immersion, with the exception of Nunavut. BC's French Immersion policy states,

> French Immersion programming benefits the cognitive and social development of students, as well as their opportunities for career advancement. Research demonstrates that students who successfully complete a French Immersion program attain functional bilingualism while doing as well as, or better than, their unilingual peers in the content areas of curriculum, including English Language Arts.[33]

Some governments recognize French Immersion but do not have provincial policies. Instead, school districts are responsible for administering French Immersion. Some districts also offer Extended French programs. These programs offer more French instruction than English-language programs but less than what is offered in French Immersion programs.

French Immersion programs may exist in the same schools as English programs, creating dual tracks, or they may be found in schools that exclusively offer French Immersion. Kids can usually enter the program at set points in their educational studies. In Manitoba, for example, kids can enter in kindergarten or grade 1, in grade 4, or in grade 7.[34] Not all districts offer French Immersion, however. Districts may accept students from outside their boundaries if their policies allow it and space exists in their programs.

Demand for French Immersion is high and growing in many parts of the country. In fact, districts sometimes can't find enough qualified teachers to teach in the programs. Enrolment statistics reported by Canadian Parents for French, a national organization that promotes French second-language learning opportunities for Canadian children, showed that 11.7 per cent of Canadian students were in French Immersion programs in 2019–20, up slightly from a few years earlier.[35] In some places the demand cannot keep up with the supply, so districts limit the number of students who can enrol. Tracy Sherlock of the *Vancouver Sun* reported that families lined up for three days in Salmon Arm, BC, to secure one of twelve coveted spots distributed on a first-come first-served basis.[36] Other districts use lotteries to determine who gets a spot. While seemingly more fair since not everyone can leave home and work for days, this arrangement left Paul Alexandre, a French-as-a-first-language speaker, fuming when his four-year-old son didn't secure a place in Brandon, MB's only single-track French Immersion school.[37] Alexandre argued his language-protection rights were violated since his son was not guaranteed instruction in French. The board offered his son a spot in other schools, but their programs offered less instructional time in French. The nearest school in the French-language board was thirty kilometres away.

The inability of all children to access French Immersion programs is a problem for the public school ideal. Policies that attempt to ensure kids from all backgrounds have a fair chance in enrolling, such as lotteries, recognize this issue. Nevertheless, French Immersion classrooms are often filled with children from advantaged backgrounds. In the TDSB, for example, there is an overrepresentation of white children, children from high income families, and students born in Canada.[38] There is also an underrepresentation of students from all other racial backgrounds (with the exception of mixed backgrounds) and students with special education needs.[39] The Ottawa-Carleton District School Board (OCDSB) reports similar patterns of enrolment. In this board, the demand for French Immersion is so high (72 per cent in 2017–18) that kids in the English track are sometimes unable to attend their local schools.[40] French Immersion programs in the OCDSB have a disproportionately lower number of students with special education needs, English language learners, and children from low income backgrounds. The lower numbers in the English program also mean more split grades and potentially less robust programming for these kids. Finally, as a 2019 OCDSB report on its English programs states, "The intersectionality of single-tracked ENG [English] schools located in low income neighborhoods, with a student body with high ELL and special education needs results in student outcomes that are not as successful as District and/or provincial norms."[41]

The location of French Immersion programs may both reflect and contribute to the problem. Researchers Gillian Parekh, Isobel Killoran, and Cameron Crawford mapped French Immersion programs in the TDSB onto the city's neighbourhoods.[42] They found that the majority of high schools offering them are found in the city's more affluent neighbourhoods (70 per cent) rather than in low income areas (30 per cent).

So why is French Immersion in such high demand? Well, first, as referenced in BC's French Immersion policy, there are many noted benefits to French Immersion, including bilingualism, better job prospects, and cognitive and social benefits. Recognizing that people in leadership positions in Canada must be bilingual, parents may select French Immersion as a way to accrue economic and symbolic capital. Also, parents may be attracted to French Immersion precisely *because* these programs typically have lower numbers of kids with special education needs, ELLs, or children with low levels of achievement. They may believe their kids will get a better experience than if they were in a "regular" English-language program with a broader range of students. Indeed, based on interviews with white anglophone middle-class parents in the Grandview-Woodlands neighbourhood in Vancouver, researchers Ee-Seul Yoon and Kalervo Gulson show that these parents put their children in French Immersion as a way to keep their kids separate from children who speak languages other than English or French.[43] Indeed, families are sometimes discouraged from putting their kids in French Immersion if they are ELLs or are struggling academically in the English program.[44] In fact, research shows these kids struggle equally whether they are in French Immersion or not.

The net result is that French Immersion programs tend to be places where white, financially secure, and academically achieving students congregate, separate from their racialized, low income, English-language-learning, or low-achieving peers. This is a problem because these spaces reproduce social patterns of advantage and disadvantage. As I discussed above, kids in homogenous classrooms miss out on opportunities to learn from children unlike themselves – this is bad for them and bad for the public interest.

E-Learning

Another option available to some students – when they are not in the midst of a global pandemic – is to take courses online through public or private schools. In some places students might choose to take one or two courses alongside their face-to-face courses (called supplementary e-learning), while in other cases, students' entire programs might be completed online. Online courses may be designed and managed at the district or provincial/territorial level, depending on the province/territory. E-learning is not an option for kids without the required technology or reliable Internet access, of course.

Dr. Beyhan Farhadi conducted a study of supplementary e-learning in the TDSB for her doctoral research.[45] She interviewed twenty students and thirty adults connected to the board's program, observed seven online courses, took field notes on the content of years of course discussions, and examined TDSB data related to achievement, gender, course allocation, and home school enrolment. Among many findings, Farhadi's analysis revealed that between 2010 and 2017, the majority of students who took e-learning courses were concentrated in only 12 (out of a possible 112) schools; these schools face low levels of external challenges (e.g., poverty, lone-parent families) compared to other schools in the board. Three of them offer a specialized program or are arts-focused schools. Conversely, only 5.9 per cent of students from the 15 schools deemed by the board to experience the highest levels of external challenges took supplementary e-learning courses during this time. In addition, the majority of courses offered through e-learning were targeted towards students aiming to go to university, and students formally identified as gifted were overrepresented in the groups of students taking them. Thus, supplementary e-learning in the TDSB primarily serves students who experience success in face-to-face classrooms and come from more advantaged backgrounds. This disproportionality, study informants at the board revealed, is partly a consequence of affluent families advocating for online courses to be available for their children.

Students Farhadi interviewed reported that the e-learning courses were easier than face-to-face ones, which meant they could get higher grades. Indeed, her observations showed that students spent far less time online than required in face-to-face classes. Since students could log on when it suited them, online courses also gave them time to pursue extracurricular activities they believed would give them an advantage when applying to university. Online courses also enabled them to avoid activities that they disliked that are common in face-to-face classes, including working with other students in groups or making presentations. For some kids, e-learning meant they could avoid difficult social situations at school. Farhadi's study shows that already advantaged students in the TDSB use supplementary e-learning as a strategy to accrue individual benefits (i.e., higher grades, extracurricular experiences) that they can use to secure advantage in competitions for university acceptances.

Like Ontario, BC's Ministry of Education and Training supports online learning (called distributive learning prior to 2021). BC's online learning model enables students to "connect with their BC-certified teacher from anywhere using the Internet, phone or mail."[46] Online courses are offered by both public and private online schools in the province. Enrolment in distributed learning programs in public schools has been steady since 2004–5.[47] However, it rose in independent schools during the same time. In 2017, about 10 per cent of kids in private schools were enrolled in distributed learning programs. Reporting in 2018, the BCTF pointed out that distributed learning was increasingly taken up by kids with special education needs, attributing this growth to the fact that the government gives private schools funding for specific students.[48] The schools, in turn, often used the money to hire an educational assistant (EA) to work with the student and may have involved their parents in hiring decisions and directing the EA's work. Thus, parents may have felt greater control over their kids' experiences and believed their child was getting better service than they would have received if they attended public schools, where funding for kids with special education needs is used to support all kids in the district.

When I started writing this chapter in late 2019 I'd planned to talk in this section about differences between optional and mandatory e-learning. At that time Ontario was poised to become unique in Canada with its new requirement that, beginning with the graduating class of 2023–4, students would be required take two courses online.[49] Detractors pointed out that lots of children don't have Internet access and warned that many students' needs, especially those of kids with exceptionalities, could not be met through online learning. They also argued there was little research showing online learning offers greater educational benefits to students than face-to-face classes. Indeed, a study of mandatory e-learning in Michigan, where students must take one course online, found only 55 per cent of kids passed online courses. This report also reveals that the pass rate for students in poverty is almost 20 per cent less than kids not in poverty.[50] It also concludes that students who struggle in regular classes will also struggle in online courses *"unless* there are appropriate support systems in place to help these students succeed" [emphasis in original].[51]

And then the COVID-19 pandemic hit, shutting down schools across the country. Suddenly, almost everyone faced the prospect of e-learning, and the concerns raised by opponents to Ontario's policy of mandatory e-learning turned into lived experiences for many students and their families. First, there was the problem of access to technology and the Internet. Many kids didn't have access to either. The Anglophone South School District in New Brunswick, for example, reported that 11 per cent of its students couldn't access online learning because they didn't have a device or Internet access; some students and their families couldn't be reached at all.[52] In response, school boards struggled to distribute Chromebooks and iPads with prepaid Internet access. Ontario's Peel District School Board reported receiving more than 20,000 requests for technology that could help kids learn at home.[53] Just having a connected device wasn't enough, however. It was clear that many kids needed an adult around to oversee their efforts to learn at home. And parents and students reported that supports for students with special needs were inadequate. Of course, some families were able to help their kids, but many found it impossible. The experience also showed that teachers need specialized training in effective online pedagogies. Teaching and learning from home demands knowledge, skills, support, and resources substantially different from what is needed in schools.

To be fair, most detractors and supporters of e-learning agree that the kind of instruction taking place online during the pandemic was better characterized as emergency remote learning rather than the kind of teaching envisioned by e-learning advocates. Nevertheless, people around the world confronted the challenges that e-learning – this supposed choice in a non-pandemic world – raised for public education. Like the other choice options I've discussed so far, e-learning is not a an option for many students and families.

All the education options I've reviewed above are choices that may be found within "traditional" public school systems. I've presented substantial evidence to support Canadian researchers Lynn Bosetti and Michael Pyryt's conclusion:

> The greatest weakness of this model of public school choice is that it privileges middle-class parents who have the social and cultural capital to navigate their way through the school selection process and those parents who have the time and necessary capabilities to organize groups to lobby for the establishment of particular alternative programs.[54]

I turn now to look at choices outside traditional public schools: charter schools, private schools, and homeschooling.

Charter Schools

Charter schools are a variation of public schools: they receive the same funding but are governed and operated by a corporate body called a charter board. Each school has a charter that outlines its unique educational offering, operating procedures, and expected student outcomes. The New Horizons School Charter, for example, states that the "New Horizons School will enable gifted students to strive for excellence in a positive academic learning environment that fosters social and emotional support for each student."[55] A charter is an agreement between the Ministry of Education and the school's founders. Alberta is the only province in Canada that has charter schools. They were introduced in the province in 1994 as part of a reform agenda that also included a 12 per cent cut to public schools, changes to district and school governance, and the provincial government taking total control of education funding.[56] Charter schools were expected to provide the same basic education as regular public schools but in a different or enhanced way. They were also expected to expand competition and school choice in Alberta, improve student achievement, and be sites of innovation and research.[57] Alberta's *Charter School Handbook* explains that charter schools "represent an opportunity for successful educational practices to be recognized and adopted by other public schools for the benefit of more Albertans."[58]

Alberta's *Charter School Handbook* explains that any individual or group can apply for a charter if they have asked their local school board to offer their desired program as an alternative program. If the board can't demonstrate that it already offers such a program and is unwilling to create one, an application for a charter school may be submitted. While they have greater autonomy in governance and operations compared to traditional public schools, charter schools have some restrictions. For example, they have to follow the Alberta curriculum. They also must hire Alberta-certified teachers and a certified principal. While charter schools aren't allowed to deny students access, they aren't obligated to meet every student's needs either. They are also able to set admissions criteria and require students to apply. Westmount Charter School requires that applicants submit a psychological assessment that indicates the child is identified as gifted, for example. The tests, which can cost hundreds of dollars or more, must be paid for by parents. Charter schools can also charge fees (as can regular public schools) and are not required to provide transportation, although they may share the costs with parents.

As of January 2020, Alberta had thirteen charter boards operating twenty-two charter schools. The schools' programs range from an arts academy to one focused on offering the Suzuki approach to learning instruments, to a school exclusively for children identified as gifted. In 2019–20 charter schools served 1.3 per cent of the province's children attending schools.[59] Since the election of the United Conservative Party (UCP) in 2019, the charter school landscape has been shifting in Alberta. When charter schools were first introduced, for example, the number of charter boards allowed in the province was fifteen. This cap was removed in 2019. In 2020, the UCP government proposed more changes, such as allowing potential charter school operators to apply directly to the minister of education for approval to begin the process to establish a new charter school. As I explained above, previously would-be operators first had to approach the local school board and ask it to establish an alternative program. Only if the board refused could a charter school be established.

Indeed, as Lynn Bosetti and Phil Butterfield argue, charter schools have put pressure on Alberta's public school boards to expand schooling options in response to parent demand as their introduction intended.[60] However, they argue that the promise that charter schools would force all schools to improve teaching and learning and adopt innovative practices has not been realized. This may be due in part to the limited number of charter schools in the province. The removal of the cap on the number of charter schools stands to address this issue. However, Bosetti and Butterfield point out that this outcome may also reflect school boards' disinterest in supporting and collaborating with charter schools as well as the challenge of scaling up successful programs. In fact, research on charter schools' impact on student achievement in the United States, while mixed, generally finds that students in charters schools do no better academically than kids in regular public schools. However, they do segregate kids along race and class lines and sometimes leave poor and racialized students in schools with fewer resources and lower academic achievement.[61]

Private Schools

Private schools are a long-standing educational choice in Canada. In fact, some Canadian private schools are older than the country itself. When you think about private schools you may picture elite institutions with high tuition, tough academic standards, and an exclusive, rich clientele. These schools certainly exist, but they are only one kind of private school. Many are small, and many are faith based. Others may be grounded in a particular teaching philosophy, such as the Montessori or Waldorf approaches. Provincial governments have vastly different laws and regulations related to private schools. In Ontario, for example, independent schools are not regulated by the Ministry of Education at all unless they wish to grant secondary school credits that can be put towards an Ontario secondary school diploma. In these cases, private schools volunteer for government review of their offerings. Private schools are subject to more restrictions in other provinces.

While private schools are part of today's educational landscape, their existence can't be attributed to efforts to create markets. However, there are policies that make it easier for some parents to choose private schools for their children. In fact, five provinces currently provide some public funding directly to private schools: BC, Alberta, Saskatchewan, Manitoba, and Quebec. I'll say more about these policies below, but I first want to recognize that some people would disagree with my decision to point to these policies as evidence of privatization.

For one thing, policies to fund private schools with public funds in BC, Alberta, Manitoba, and Quebec predate the contemporary trend towards education privatization. Researchers often point to the late 1970s and early 1980s as the time when governments began introducing policies reflecting neoliberal ideals.[62] And while the first policy to fund private schools with public money was introduced in BC in 1977, debates over the funding issue have a much longer history.[63] Thus, the policy might "count" as privatization only under certain conditions. You might call it privatization if the amount of public funding given to private schools has increased at a faster rate than the amounts given to public education. This is what the BCTF argues has been the case in BC.[64] Using the BC Ministry of Education's data, the BCTF reports that the growth in inflation-adjusted funding from 2000–1 to 2019–20 was 122.8 per cent for private schools and just 15.9 per cent for the province's public schools. The BCTF attributes this difference to increases in enrolment in private schools as well as changing funding policies (e.g., private schools now receive the same amount of funding for some students with special needs as public schools). Alternatively, you might point to the policy as evidence of privatization if the amount of funding given to private schools has increased over time. This is what has happened in Alberta.[65] In 1967, the province gave a hundred dollars per student per year to private schools that met the government's conditions. In 1974, the amount was increased to 33 per cent of the amount public school boards received per student; in 1976 it was 40 per cent. By 1998, the amount most private schools received was 60 per cent, and since 2008 most private schools receive 70 per cent of what public schools get per student

Some people actually argue that private schools that accept public money become *more public* if there are strings attached to the funds. Historian Jean Barman argued that BC's decision to partially fund private schools has ultimately resulted in the province's private schools becoming deprivatized.[66] In its first iteration in 1977, the legislation required that private schools that wanted to receive 10 per cent of what public schools received per child had to convince school inspectors that they had appropriate facilities and did not promote religious or racial intolerance or societal change through violence. Schools that wanted to receive 30 per cent had to operate as non-profit organizations, offer the same basic program of education as public schools, employ qualified teachers, and participate in the province's student examination and assessment programs. Later changes to the legislation included the ability of schools that met all the requirements of the public school system and whose per-pupil operating costs were no higher than those of the public system to receive 50 per cent of what public schools received per student. Schools with per-pupil operating costs higher than public schools could still receive 35 per cent. The lowest funded schools could still obtain 10 per cent of public schools costs per student, but they too now had to provide an educational program aligned with that provided in public schools. The Independent School Act of 1989 put all private schools under government control; explicitly forbade them from promoting ethnic or racial superiority, religious intolerance, or the use of violence to bring about social change; and committed all schools to pursuing the social and economic purposes of the province. With these changes, Barman concluded, "British Columbia's remaining 'private' schools were in effect legislated out of existence."[67]

I can see Barman's point: schools that accept public funds with strings attached do give up some of their autonomy. Nevertheless even private schools that accept public money and follow government guidelines remain far from the public school ideal.

Five provinces currently provide some public funding directly to private schools: BC, Alberta, Saskatchewan, Manitoba, and Quebec. It's not easy to figure out exactly how much schools get since there are normally multiple funding streams (e.g., capital expenses, transportation costs; special education grants). Typically, the base amount private schools receive depends on the per-student amount funded in public schools. As you can see in Table 3, the provinces allocate different amounts per funded public school student (from 50 per cent to 80 per cent), and some differentiate how much various types of private schools receive. In BC, for example, there are two groups of schools that receive public funding. Group 1 schools are those whose per-student operating costs do not exceed those of local school districts; they get 50 per cent per student of what public schools get per student. Group 2 schools have per-student operating costs greater than local districts, and they receive per-student grants equal to 35 per cent of those received by public schools.

All provinces require that private schools that receive public funds meet certain conditions. These conditions may include hiring teachers certified by province, requiring students to take provincial tests, using provincial curriculum, being operated by a non-profit organization, and others. Note that the funding is given to the school rather than the students or their parents. Every province has some schools that choose not to receive public funds and in so doing retain more autonomy.

There are other ways parents who send their children to private schools receive public subsidies for their choices, even in provinces without formal funding to schools. Revenue Canada permits parents whose children attend faith-based private schools registered as charities to have a portion of their schools' tuition considered a donation, and thus, receive a charitable receipt for the amount.[68] If a family member or person other than a child's parent or guardian pays the tuition, they can count the full amount as a donation. Parents can also claim a childcare deduction for non-instructional

Table 3. Approximate Base Funding Per Student Allocated to Private Schools

Province	Approximate Base Funding Per Student Allocated to Private Schools
BC	Group 1 schools: 50%
	Group 2 schools: 35%
AB	Level 1: 60%
	Level 2: 70%
SK*	Associate schools: 80%
	Historical high schools: 70%
	Qualified independent schools: 50%
MB	50% of public school operating costs from two years previous
QC	60%

Source: Lynn Bosetti, Deani Van Pelt, and Derek J. Allison, "The Changing Landscape of School Choice in Canada: From Pluralism to Parental Preference?" *Education Policy Analysis Archives* 25, no. 38 (April 2017): 16.
* Saskatchewan also funds alternative independent schools through individual service agreements. These schools serve students with special education needs.

parts of their kids' time at school. Private school costs may also be subsidized indirectly through municipal tax exemptions.

Some opponents of public funding of private schools argue that the policies encourage privatization by enabling more parents to take up this option. Stéphane Vigneault, member of Quebec's Mouvement L'école ensemble, a group advocating for more equitable public schooling, attributes the growth in student enrolment in the province's private schools between 1970 and 2020 (from 5 per cent to 22 per cent) to the introduction of public funding of private schools in 1968.

Policies that fund private schools with public dollars don't benefit everyone, and they certainly don't support the public school ideal. To begin, families with high incomes are more likely to choose private schools than those with low incomes; thus, the ones who need public subsidies are less likely to use them.[69] Further, private schools still charge some tuition as none of the provinces that fund private schools cover every expense. For kids whose families can't afford these costs, private schools with some government funding remain out of reach. And, as scholar Jerry Paquette argues, given the importance of education to individuals' future outcomes, it's unethical to expect individuals from lower income backgrounds to pay taxes used to subsidize private schools when these individuals and their families are the least likely to use them.[70]

Let's say for a minute that money was not an issue, that everyone could afford the costs of private schools. Another problem related to access remains. Private schools are able to select their students according to their own criteria. Unlike public schools, private schools can turn students away who don't "fit" for some reason: they may have special education needs, struggle academically, speak a language other than English or French, or express values different from those espoused by the school. I understand that there are some private schools that serve children with special needs; I'm not talking about these schools. Kids who are excluded from private schools, who in some cases may be harder or more expensive to educate, won't reap the same benefits from the policy as those who attend private schools. Those who remain in public schools do so without the diversity of kids that might have otherwise been there. Both groups miss out on learning from the other.

There have been other initiatives aimed at making it easier for parents to choose private schools introduced in the past few decades. In 2001 in Ontario, for example, Mike Harris's Progressive Conservative government introduced the Equity in Education tax credit. Once fully implemented, parents would've been able to claim up to half of the education portion of private school tuition up to a maximum of $3,500. Reaction to the tax credit was mixed. Some opponents, including teacher unions, some school boards, and some parent groups, viewed the tax credit as an incentive for parents to enrol their children in private schools. When the Liberal government under Dalton McGuinty was elected in 2003, it fulfilled a campaign promise and promptly cancelled the tax credit. The tax-break plan resurfaced in 2017 when Conservative Party of Canada's Andrew Scheer promised to introduce federal tax credits to parents who send their children to private schools as part of his bid for party leader. He ultimately dropped this commitment before the 2019 federal election, however, citing the size of the country's budget deficit.

Advocates of school choice have also floated vouchers as a way to enable more parents to choose private schools for their kids. In this approach funding for the cost of educating a student is given directly to a student's family in the form of a voucher that they can use to pay full or partial tuition for the school of their choice. The vouchers may be given to all children or may be targeted to particular populations so that they may participate in education markets. Voucher programs exist in many US states and in other countries around the world.[71] A targeted voucher initiative, Children First: School Choice Trust, existed in Ontario and Alberta between 2003 and 2012.[72] It was a program of Canada's Fraser Institute, an organization that advocates "the redirection of public attention to the role of competitive markets in providing for the well-being of Canadians."[73] While not a voucher in the traditional sense since funds were provided by private donors rather than governments, the Children First program provided tuition grants to parents with low incomes to enable them to access private schools. The grants covered up to 50 per cent of a school's tuition cost, up to a maximum amount that varied over the life of the program. At its highest point, the voucher covered up to $3,500.

The director of the Children First: School Choice Trust surveyed grant recipients in the first year of the program. Two-thirds of respondents sent their children to religious schools, whereas almost 17 per cent chose Montessori and 3 per cent chose Waldorf schools. The most commonly cited reasons for choosing a private school included academic quality of the school (87 per cent), values taught at the school (78 per cent), class sizes (65 per cent), and religious reasons (56 per cent). After just a few months in the new schools, the majority of parents reported their children's academic achievement, social skills, and behaviour had improved. Ninety-one per cent said their children were happier. While these findings sound great, you have to wonder whether parents could give anything but positive feedback to the group helping to pay for their children's schooling. Also, there were no follow-up studies, so the impact of the program is unknown. Children First: School Choice Trust ended in 2012.

While parents of kids participating in the Children First: School Choice Trust may have reported academic improvements, research on outcomes of voucher schemes in other places in the world suggests the impact on student achievement is modest at best.[74] A lot of studies don't find any impact on grades at all, and some even find a negative impact.[75] However, voucher programs, like other school choice mechanisms, tend to increase segregation between schools along socioeconomic, ethnic, and ability lines.[76] Nevertheless, advocates of school vouchers remain. In late 2019, members of Alberta's United Conservative Party passed a resolution to "[i]mplement an education 'voucher system' that will provide for equal per-student funding regardless of their school choice, free from caveats or conditions."[77]

Homeschooling

I'm not going to spend a lot of time on homeschooling. Some might say it isn't an example of privatization because it has always existed in Canada. It was once the only form of education many kids had. Today homeschooling refers to parents taking full responsibility for their kids' education in contexts in which children could otherwise go to public or private schools. It also differs from most of the other forms of school choice I've discussed in this chapter because, as Aurini and Davies argue, homeschooling does not provide kids with any obvious economic benefits, competitive advantages, or means of securing class status that the other choices discussed above do.[78]

However, it *is* an option in Canada's education marketplace. With rates ranging from a low of 0.2 per cent in Quebec and in Newfoundland and Labrador in 2016-17 to a high of 2.8 per cent in the Yukon, it isn't a particularly popular choice.[79] Nevertheless, the phenomenon is growing in Canada; the number of kids homeschooled increased by just over 29 per cent between 2006–7 and 2011–12.[80] The number of kids homeschooled in Canada might actually be higher as not all parents register their children.

Homeschooling is allowed in all provinces and territories, and all governments require that parents inform some authority (a school, school board or government) in more or less formal ways. In Ontario, for example, parents only need to inform their local school board each year before 1 September.[81] Next door in Quebec, however, not only do parents have to report their intention to homeschool to their local school board and the minister of education, they also have to submit formal learning plans that align with the government's education program, produce midterm reports on the implementation of the learning plan and their children's progress, attend a monitoring meeting with a representative of the minister during the implementation of the plans, and assess and report their children's progress to the minister by 15 June.[82] The Canadian Home Based Learning group, a support group for homeschooling parents, calls Quebec one of the "least homeschool-friendly provinces in Canada."[83]

Not surprisingly, perhaps, Quebec doesn't provide funding to homeschooling parents. In fact, most provinces don't. A few do, however. In Alberta, parents can be reimbursed for some of the cost of instructional materials and resources. In 2017–18 the amount parents could receive was about $835. In BC, funds for kids who are homeschooled go to the school boards and independent schools where they are registered. In Saskatchewan, policies vary by school district. Whether or not a child can earn a provincial or territorial diploma also varies: in BC they can't, but in Quebec they can, for example.

Given the responsibility and work of homeschooling, why do parents do it? After the introduction of mass schooling, homeschoolers were from two main groups: religious fundamentalists or parents who rejected the rigidity and conformity of educational institutions.[84] This second group were often followers of John Holt and members of the unschooling movement. Parents' reasons for homeschooling are changing, however. Reporting in 2003 on findings from their interviews with homeschooling parents in Ontario, Scott Davies and Janice Aurini explain that contemporary parents' main reasons for making this choice included their desire to "give their child a tailored educational experience, or maintain the integrity of their family unit."[85] That is, many homeschooling parents see today's public schools as too depersonalized and are looking for an education that will enhance their children's unique talents and learning needs. Some parents also reported that homeschooling enabled them to pass on their personal values (although these were not necessarily based on religion).

Importantly, research in the United States finds that African American families may turn to homeschooling for another reason: to remove their children from schools where they face anti-Black racism, bullying, and systemic racism.[86] The same appears to be true for some Black families in Canada as well. While their exact numbers aren't available, homeschooling Black parents in Canada report they turned to homeschooling so their children could avoid the harm many Black children in public schools experience, including harsher punishments, higher rates of suspension and expulsion, and overrepresentation in special education and lower academic streams.[87] Indeed, given the anti-Black racism that exists in schools, these parents may have few other options. When Black parents engage with schools they are regularly subjected to negative stereotypes and other forms of anti-Black racism.[88]

Removing one's own children as a form of protest is an understandable response to systemic racism in public schools. Eliminating anti-Black racism in public education demands, at minimum, rewriting curriculum and pedagogy, nurturing Black identities, challenging stereotypes, changing policies and structures that exclude Black children – including the ones I discuss in this book.[89] This work requires that everyone acknowledge the ways norms of whiteness uphold white privilege in schools and society.[90] In the public school ideal, all children have the same opportunity to reap the benefits of public schooling. There is no doubt that public schools in Canada have a long way to go before Black, Indigenous, racialized, disabled, and other groups of marginalized children have this opportunity.

Yet homeschooling will not bring us closer to realizing the public school ideal. Homeschooled children may benefit from more personalized learning, opportunities to pursue other interests, and hospitable learning environments, but they miss the chance to learn about children who remain in public schools, children who may be very different from them, but with whom they must live and work. The same is true for the kids enrolled in public school: they don't get to know their homeschooled peers. In provinces that provide funding to homeschooling parents, there is another worry for the public school ideal. The funds can be used to buy books and curriculum resources that have not been vetted by governments or the school board; that is, they have not been subjected to any form of public decision-making.[91] It's possible the materials contain ideas that the Canadian public would not want to support. In addition, the money going out to homeschooling parents is money that might otherwise be spent in public schools that many children could access. Finally, like other school choice alternatives, homeschooling is not an option that all families can choose. It is available only to those who have a parent or other adult who can teach the child(ren). Many families simply aren't able to afford to make this choice. For these reasons public schools must be welcoming places where all children can be successful.

Segregation and Stratification

Taken together, the above discussion shows that school choice policies in Canada tend to segregate and stratify. This conclusion reflects research findings about school choice in other places as well, including many US states, the UK, Australia, New Zealand, and Chile.[92] So what should we do about school choice?

To begin, I don't believe the public should fund homeschooling or private schools. I say this mainly because these options aren't available to everyone. In some cases this is due to finances. Private schools, however, can also exclude kids based on their admission criteria. Homeschooling, on the other hand, is available only to families with an adult able to actually provide instruction, and the materials and methods used aren't subject to public oversight. Depending on the policy, this can also be the case for private schools. I recognize that some families choose homeschooling or private schools because they've faced discrimination or rejection from traditional public schools. The solution isn't to enable some of those kids to exit while others remain. Instead, public schools have to do better.

When it comes to other school choice policies, there are a few options. None of them are certain to achieve the public school ideal. Some move us closer to it than others, however. One approach is to maintain existing schools and programs and improve access to them and their benefits. To begin, there can't be any fees associated with choosing the school or program (and no, fee waivers won't suffice). Of course, transportation will also have to be available and free for all students. There also can't be any entrance requirements or complicated application processes that give advantages to families with more social, political, and financial capital. Given that a rationale for many specialized schools and programs is that they enable kids to pursue their interests alongside or as a vehicle for meeting curriculum requirements, the only requirement to attend should be *interest*. If more kids express interest than there are spots available, a few responses are possible. One idea is to offer admission first to kids not faring well in traditional school programs or those schools have historically underserved: typically, kids who are poor, Black, Indigenous, and/or have special needs. Another idea is to make more spots available so that everyone who wants one gets one. Or a lottery system could be used to determine who gets in. At minimum, school choice policies must explicitly attempt to ensure schools of choice are racially and socioeconomically diverse. If they don't, research shows the policies increase stratification and separation of kids by race and ethnicity.[93]

I anticipate that these options won't sit well with some parents and students, many of whom will argue that a specialized school or program's quality will be compromised if they let just anyone in. But this argument reveals its proponents' belief that the program is only as good as it is precisely *because* it excludes others. Why should public schools offer better programs to some kids and not others (especially when the kids in these programs often do well in regular school programs)? And why should the public pay for them?

Even if districts take these steps, their schools and programs should be subject to regular audits wherein classrooms, schools, and teacher behaviours are evaluated to determine if they are equitable.[94] The student body should also be examined to determine whether it reflects the wider demographics of the district. If not, all facets of the program, including recruitment, admissions, practices, and curriculum need to be considered as possible points of exclusion, segregation, and stratification.

Even if districts adopt all the strategies outlined above, we can bet that there will still be families and kids that can't or won't participate in school choice. I also suspect it would be logistically and financially difficult, if not impossible, to ensure the supply of specialty schools and programs can meet the demand for them. A better alternative is to ensure every public school offers excellent academic programming, is fully resourced, and welcomes all kids from its neighbourhood. Ideally, its student body would reflect the diversity of society. I know, of course, that more than education policy will have to change before this can be achieved, but it's a goal we must pursue.

Securing Advantages in Public Education Using Private Means: Beyond Fundraising and School Choice

So far I've focused on how fundraising and school choice policies enable some parents to secure private benefits for their kids in public schools, but they do so through other means as well. In each case I discuss below – private assessments, tutoring, and single course credits – parents who can afford it pay for services outside of public education systems that result in individual advantages for their children inside public schools.

One way this happens is when parents pay out of pocket for psychological testing using a private provider. They do this because they (and maybe teachers or others) suspect their child might have a need that can be met only through a modified educational program or learning environment. Their concerns might include a learning disability, giftedness, or some other exceptionality. In Ontario, parents or teachers can bring their concerns to a special committee at the school, which, if in agreement, can recommend that the child be tested to confirm and possibly diagnose a problem. In many Ontario schools districts, however, there are long waiting lists for publicly funded psychological testing. The wait can be years long for a number of reasons, including inadequate government funding of psychologists and others who can perform the tests in public school systems; the unavailability or limited number of psychologists in a particular geographical location (wait lists are shorter in big cities); district policies that limit testing to be done only by psychologists or other specified professionals; and the reliance on test results as a criterion for decision-making.[95]

The results of psychological tests are used by school or board committees to determine whether special education supports are needed by the student, and if so, they will be provided by the school district. Understandably, many parents don't want to wait years for their child to receive special needs supports if they are deemed necessary. So those who can afford to pay for private testing do so and bring the results to the school or board committee so decisions can be made more quickly. The problem with these practices is, of course, that not all families can afford to pay for these assessments, meaning wealthier kids jump the line and access support services more quickly than less affluent families.

Another way parents who have money use it to buy advantages for their kids is by paying for individual courses taught by private providers (as opposed to a child completing all of their schooling at a private school). There are private schools that offer students the chance to take single credits outside of their regular public school day. The courses may be offered in face-to-face, hybrid, or online formats, as well as through travel. When a student earns the credit it is posted on their public school report card, and the course grade is included in the student's final average. There may be a notation on the report card that the credit was taken someplace other than the student's regular public school. There are different reasons why kids take courses through these private providers. Some kids are looking for a way to boost their marks to be more competitive in the university application process. These schools have a reputation of being easier than regular public day schools and the grades earned there of being generally higher – hence why they are sometimes called "credit mills." One student told CBC reporters that he took four grade 12 courses at a private school for approximately $600 per course, explaining, "They would just give you the mark for free. For English, I barely showed up but ended up with a 90. Almost everyone ended up with a 90 … It was a joke."[96] Some of them have been investigated and even shut down for falsifying students' grades and attendance.[97]

University admissions officers are aware of these schools' reputations and may be suspect of grades earned through them.

However, since the schools are approved by the government, universities cannot discount them when looking at applicants' grades. I attended a presentation at an Ontario university with my son when he was applying to postsecondary institutions, and we were told that at that school grades earned in courses taken a second time would not be considered in admissions decisions. While I can't say for sure that this is a strategy to address concerns about credit mills, I couldn't help but wonder. What I find especially egregious is not only that kids with high grades obtained at single-credit private schools may secure university or college spots that they haven't earned, but they may also be awarded competitive academic scholarships. Remember the kid who told CBC that the courses he took were a joke? He landed a place in Toronto Metropolitan University's engineering program and $4,000!

Another reason kids might take single credits through private providers is the exceptional nature of the educational opportunity. There is an entire industry offering students credits through travel. Many of my sons' friends completed Ontario's required grade 10 civics and careers course over their spring break while travelling to Ottawa and Washington DC. Information about these travel-while-earning-a-credit opportunities can be found on district websites leading parents to believe they are at least endorsed by, if not provided by, the school board. In some cases, the school boards actually do partner with private providers. It's pretty easy to see how these single-credit private schools violate the public school ideal: their benefits aren't available to everyone, they aren't paid for by the government, and their decision-making isn't available for public scrutiny. While they don't claim to be public schools, the grades and experiences students accrue there count towards their public school credentials.

Finally, I want to talk briefly about private tutoring. While hiring tutors for kids struggling in a particular subject is not new, many of today's tutors work in individual franchises of comprehensive "learning centres" such as Oxford Learning and Sylvan Learning. Janice Aurini and Scott Davies distinguish between two types of tutoring services.[98] The first type, shadow education, refers to individual tutors who generally work alone and follow the local public school system's curricula. They offer homework help and test preparation to help kids improve their grades or do well on an upcoming assessment. Learning centres, on the other hand, are businesses that use their own curriculum to develop skills that will be useful to students in the long term, such as study skills, note taking, and reading comprehension. Oxford Learning's website, for example, explains,

> With Oxford Learning®'s programs you'll be putting an end to the time and expense of hiring a tutor year after year – instead, you'll be giving your child the skills he or she needs to deal with today's school struggles, and helping him or her develop thinking and learning skills that will be used for this grade and for every grade.[99]

Kumon's website, similarly, states,

> Kumon goes beyond tutoring. Instead, children actively develop critical thinking skills while progressing independently through a carefully crafted, Kumon curriculum. The Kumon Math program covers everything from counting to calculus. The worksheets enable children to learn new concepts on their own.[100]

Learning centres may still offer homework assistance, but it is not their only focus. Instead, they offer series of lessons in subject and skill areas, usually placing students in programs based on their own assessments rather than according to age, grade, or school marks.

Writing in 2004, Aurini and Davies predicted that tutoring businesses, including learning centres, would continue to grow despite a lack of conclusive evidence that tutoring impacts student achievement. They expected this would happen in part due to a generalized culture of competition in Ontario derived from the belief that education is the means to secure or advance one's socioeconomic position. They weren't wrong; tutoring businesses have expanded across the country and are poised to grow even more due to the COVID-19 pandemic.[101] Parents and students continue to seek ways to manage risk and, hopefully, gain advantage in the competitive arena, and they look to tutoring as a way to do so.

A friend of mine suggested another reason parents might enrol their kids in a tutoring service. She explained that when her daughter was in middle school she began struggling in math and claimed, for the first time, to hate it. My friend observed her daughter feeling bad about herself and worried she would turn away from math (or as she put it, she "saw her daughter becoming a statistic"). Instead, she wanted her daughter to see herself as someone who does math. So she turned to the Math Guru. According to the Math Guru's website,

> Anyone can do well at math and science. Students simply need a teacher who can communicate with them in a language that they understand; a teacher who can get them excited about learning and understanding; a teacher that can inspire them to build the confidence they need to finally understand that they've got what it takes to GET IT![102]

Indeed, as my friend explained, she hoped the Math Guru would do more than improve her daughter's grades: she hoped they would build her daughter's self-esteem. And they did.

What this story suggests is that parents who can afford tutoring are buying more than just skills. They are also paying for intangibles such as moral support and confidence. Believing in yourself as well as having others' confidence in you are two more private goods, and both can be drawn upon to support academic success in school.

Paying for tutoring, private psychological assessments, or individual high school credits, are just three ways parents can use their private resources to buy advantages for their children outside the classroom that impact their own – and others' – opportunities inside public schools. I've yet to see a special education placement, university application, or grading policy that takes these external resources into account. Instead, all kids are evaluated against the same standard or each other, even though some clearly have advantages over others. How unfair.

I point to these parental practices and outcomes of school choice policies not to vilify parents who want their children to succeed in school and after graduation. However, I want them to understand how their individual choices are connected to the patterns of in-equality in our society. By choosing an arts-focused program, for example, a parent is not only enabling their child to have their schooling experiences tailored to their interests and strengths, they are also contributing to racially and socioeconomically segregated schools. Yes, their child may thrive, but their success may come at a cost to other kids – and to the strong democratic society many Canadians claim to want to live in. But the solution is not to ex-pect that individual parents should refuse to enrol their kids in programs and schools they believe to be best for their children. Others will step in to take their spots. Instead, as citizens we have to demand more from our policymakers who have introduced pol-icies that maybe they believed would serve the public interest but instead have enabled our country's most advantaged parents to ensure their advantages are passed on to the next generation. In the next and final chapter I discuss what you can do to challenge growing privatization in Canada and strive towards the public school ideal.

chapter five

Taking Action

"All Out For Our KIDS! All Out For Public Education!" implored East End Parents 4 Public Education on its Facebook page. Like other groups around the province, East End Parents formed to protest policies introduced by Doug Ford's PC government in Ontario. This call to action, originally posted by the Ontario Parent Action Network and Ontario Families for Public Education, implored parents to join education workers in a picket line around Queen's Park on 21 February 2020. The province's four teachers unions planned to strike that day – the first united action of the unions in more than twenty years. Volunteers would offer free day camps to make it possible for more parents to attend the rally and support teachers. East End Parents 4 Public Education's Facebook post practically shouted,

We will fiercely defend all our kids!
Reverse all cuts & harmful changes!
Settle a fair deal for our kids and our ed workers now!!

East End Parents 4 Public Education surely weren't disappointed. Thirty-thousand education workers and countless supporters showed up on that cold, sunny day to demand that the government back down on its new e-learning and class-size policies, cuts to education services, and a legislated 1 per cent cap on salary increases.[1] Kids and adults sang songs and carried signs, many of them playful but poignant: "I'm using my teacher voice now: class size matters!"[2] Others pointed to a direct link between the government's policies and private sector interests: "Ontario

Education is not a business";[3] *"Education cuts lead to privatization and quality education only for the rich"*;[4] *"Privatization is THEFT!"*[5]

A press conference with the heads of the Ontario English Catholic Teachers' Association, the Ontario Secondary School Teachers' Federation (OSSTF), the Association of Franco-Ontarian Teachers, and the president of the Elementary Teachers' Federation of Ontario kicked off the rally. Harvey Bischof, president of the OSSTF, asserted, "When you have a government that plays politics with publicly funded education ... then you need to show unity, and that's what we're doing — the four education unions in a historic action, unified in defence of public education."[6]

The rally at Queen's Park was only one of many that day as education workers, parents, community members, and children demonstrated across Ontario. While there was likely more than concerns about educational privatization motivating these events – the unions were in the middle of difficult contract negotiations with the provincial government – they show that there are lots of people who value public education. Many of them are paying close attention to connections between current and proposed education policies, including online learning, funding cuts, and education privatization. You are obviously one of those people or else you wouldn't still be reading this book!

As you know by now, education privatization is a multifaceted phenomenon. It includes ideas, policies, and practices that make public education more like the private sector. The creation and expansion of education markets and the introduction of New Public Management (NPM) are two primary means of shifting the nature of public education. In chapter 2 I explained that large-scale student achievement tests, a strategy to determine education quality and value-for-money, are now common across Canada. So too are policies that encourage education markets, including open enrolment policies, specialized schools and programs, and public funding of private schools. In theory these policies may make it possible for all kids to attend schools that align with their needs and interests, but research from across Canada and beyond demonstrates that in fact the students who benefit most from them are often those from already advantaged families. Schools and specialized programs become socially stratified – all at the public's expense.

Education privatization also involves transferring responsibilities previously provided by governments to private actors. Fundraising and school fees are policies that call on parents, communities, and businesses to take on the role of education funder. The research I reviewed in chapter 3 shows that these policies often result in unequal access to resources and opportunities within public schools for both parents and children. Waiver policies designed to mitigate this situation for students depend on families knowing the policies exist and then exposing their financial situation to school staff, ignoring the stigma attached to people with low incomes. The turn to recruiting international students by school districts as a way to raise money further commodifies public education and facilitates inequality on a global scale.

Policies enabling privatization ultimately position education as primarily a private rather than a collective good. They encourage parents to do whatever they can to secure advantages for their kids – even though doing so may come at the expense of other people's children. I don't believe that most parents deliberately set out to disadvantage others, so I hope this book helps them see how policies facilitating education privatization set them up to do just that.

In this chapter I lay out some ideas for how you can participate in the struggle for strong public education. My recommendations are grounded in my commitment to critical democracy. As I explained in chapter 1, critical democracy is more than a form of government: it's a way of living together that pursues economic, social, and, political justice for all.[7] Unlike conservative or market-oriented conceptions of democracy, critical democracy prioritizes equity, inclusion, diversity, and collective participation in serving the public good.[8] It requires that education policies reflect these values; when they don't, they must be abandoned. We must, then, stop the privatization of public education and commit to creating policies that promote the public school ideal. And while we might not all be able to act in the same way, we can all do something. Indeed, critical democracy demands that we do. It is in this spirit that I offer the following ideas.

Stay Informed

I've covered a lot of ground in this book, and hopefully you know more about education privatization now than you did when you read the first page. But this is only the beginning. It's crucial that you stay informed, as knowledge about education policies and their effects is constantly changing and so is our world. Pretty much all of what I've reported in this book occurred in a place that we will never return to: the world pre-COVID-19. In that world, education privatization was facilitated in large part by neoliberalism, a set of ideas that champions competition, efficiency, meritocracy, less government, and the free market. But as an Ontario talk show, *The Agenda with Steve Paikin*, asked in May 2020, Will COVID-19 end neoliberalism? If so, what will follow? If not, will education privatization intensify?

I have no doubt that many researchers, educators, journalists, and other public education advocates will closely monitor the unfolding policy environment in an effort to answer these and other unanticipated questions. And you should too. Besides keeping up with the news, there are a number of free resources you can check out. One source is *The Conversation* (https://theconversation.com/ca), a website that publishes researched-based short articles on key issues, including education. You can also look at free academic journals that focus on education policy, including the *Canadian Journal of Educational Administration and Policy*, *Education Policy Analysis Archives* (the theme of volume 25, number 37 is "School Diversification and Dilemmas across Canada in an Era of Education Marketization and Neoliberalization"), and the *Journal for Critical Education Policy Studies*.

However, some of the most easily accessible resources are published and curated by Canadian organizations that have long resisted education privatization. One of these groups is People for Education, a public education advocacy and research organization in Ontario. It was formed by a group of parents in 1995 to protest funding cuts to education by Mike Harris's PC government. Its members were keenly aware of creeping education privatization through fundraising, school fees, and policies that allowed parents to pay for private psychological testing so their kids could access special education supports sooner than children who had to wait for publicly funded assessments. The group's earliest activities included encouraging kids to write Christmas wish lists for schools and, like the teachers described in the narrative above, organizing rallies at Queen's Park. Its members regularly participate in formal policy consultations, and its executive director is a regular commentator on education policy in the media. The group hosts an annual conference in Toronto that is attended by hundreds of people, including parents, school council members, not-for-profit organization representatives, researchers, and elected officials (often including Ontario's minister of education).

One of People for Education's most important contributions is its annual survey of Ontario's public schools. Since 1998, the group has surveyed principals in an effort to track effects of government policies. Survey findings are published in annual reports and are freely available on the group's website. Sometimes People for Education will publish special reports that hone in on an aspect of an annual report or conduct additional research on a topic of concern. These reports provide unique and essential data about privatization (and other issues) in Ontario's public education systems. You may have noticed that I referenced their numbers a lot in chapter 3; indeed, it is the only group that collects Ontario-wide data on fees and fundraising and makes it available to the public. You should definitely check out People for Education's website to access their reports and find links to education news, research, and events. You can also follow them on Twitter and Facebook and sign up for their monthly e-newsletter.

Out West, another organization is keeping a close eye on education privatization. Support our Students (SOS) Alberta describes itself as "Alberta's public education advocates, fighting for the right of all children to an equitable and accessible public education system."[9] Committed to strengthening public education in the province, the group is concerned about charter schools and other forms of education privatization as well as class sizes and underfunding. The group identifies ten strategies for strengthening public education, including eliminating all school fees, getting rid of application procedures for specialized schools, and bringing charter schools into the public system. It's also opposed to public funding of private schools.

SOS Alberta is not a lobby group but rather a citizens' action group that advocates "in public."[10] It also aims to inform Alberta's citizens about education issues and provide them with means to advocate for themselves. To this end, on its website you can find its reports on education spending and fundraising in Alberta and a tool kit with advice and strategies for influencing elected officials. SOS Alberta has also organized rallies in support of public education and hosted screenings of *Backpack Full of Cash*, a documentary that highlights the impacts of market-based education reforms in the United States as part of its efforts to inform Albertans about growing inequities and privatization in the province. The group mobilizes research and commentary about education privatization via Twitter, Facebook, and its website as well as through traditional media channels. It is another group to follow.

Adopting a national perspective, the Canadian Centre for Policy Alternative's (CCPA) Education Project monitors educational privatization across Canada. CCPA staff participate in government policy consultations and speak at conferences and events across the country. They have conducted and disseminated research on many of the topics I've discussed in this book, including vouchers, fees, fundraising, and charter schools. In fact, in 2006 the CCPA collaborated with the Canadian Teachers' Federation and Fédération des syndicats de l'enseignement to conduct the only national survey of privatization of public education in Canada to date. The survey findings are published in *Commercialism in Canadian Schools: Who's Calling the Shots?*[11] While its findings may be somewhat out of date, the report remains one of the only easily accessible sources of information about privatization in schools in many parts of the country. You can find a free copy on the CCPA's website.

The CCPA has critically examined other educational privatization policies as well, including public-private partnerships, high-stakes testing, and private sector influence on teaching and learning. In 2020, for example, affiliates from CCPA's Saskatchewan office released a report on the influence of the oil sector on the province's school curriculum. Based on original research, the report's authors detail how, contrary to accusations that public schools teach kids to be anti-oil, groups funded by the oil industry have a strong influence on lessons about climate change, energy, and the environment in the province's schools.[12] As one of few progressive think tanks in the country, the CCPA makes important contributions to policy debates about education.

The CCPA also publishes *Our Schools/Our Selves*. This journal provides a space for researchers, educators, activists, and other citizens committed to social justice to debate education-policy issues. The theme of its Winter 2020 issue was "Resisting the Neoliberal Vision of Public Education." Many of the journal's articles are free to readers; you can access them on the group's website. In 2014 *Our Schools/Our Selves* published *Privatization of Schools: Selling Out the Right to a Quality Public Education for All*, a book-length special issue. Definitely worth a read, and you can access it for free online.

Teacher unions are another source of information about privatization in education. For example, in 2016, the Canadian Teachers' Federation (CTF) published *Public Education a Public Good: Report on Privatization of K–12 Education in Canada*.[13] The report contains CTF members' and other teacher unions' observations on the prevalence of privatization and commercialization of education in their respective provinces. One of the things I find most striking in this report is the variation across the country. On the one hand, the Newfoundland and Labrador Teachers' Association stated that while "it is aware of education privatization as an issue … there is no evidence of any great push toward privatization of education in the K–12 sector in the province."[14] In BC, however, the Syndicat des enseignantes et enseignants du programme francophone de la Colombie-Britannique reports that "Privatization of K–12 education is a very big issue."[15] The report also contains the policy and position statements on privatization in education of teacher unions across the country, where they exist. Again, the diversity is striking.

There are, of course, organizations promoting educational privatization. Their resources are also worth checking out as they will help you keep track of their arguments, activities, and collaborators. The Fraser Institute is one such organization. As I mentioned in the previous chapter, this group studies and promotes market-based approaches to government policies and programs. The Fraser Institute's reports are freely available on its website and examine topics such as public funding of private schools, which families choose private schools, and school choice, including charter schools. The Atlantic Institute for Market Studies (AIMS), once an independent think tank but now affiliated with the Fraser Institute, also publishes opinion pieces and policy papers on education privatization policies such as charter schools, vouchers, and public-private partnerships. You can find these resources on the AIMS website.

Ask Critical Questions

It's useful to read others' research, but sometimes you'll want, or need, to conduct your own. Canada is a large, diverse, country. Each provincial and territorial government has its own policies. So too do districts and schools. And how people enact policy depends on their context. Quite frankly, there's a lot we don't know about how privatization is impacting our schools and communities. While we can learn from what happens in other places, research and experience tells us that each district, school, classroom, family, and community is unique. In the appendix, I explain how you might go about designing and conducting an original critical policy study. Doing so involves finding a topic, coming up with research questions, identifying theories to think with, selecting a methodology (including your data sources, data-collection strategies, and method of data analysis), carrying it out, and drawing conclusions based on what you find out. This can be a lot of work, and it may take more time, energy, and other resources than what you have on hand. It just won't be practical for everyone. But what everyone can do is raise questions central to critical policy analysis, including

- Who does this policy benefit? How?
- Who loses from the policy? How?
- How does this policy perpetuate or challenge unequal social relations?
- Why was this policy created? Who participated in its creation?

You might be able to find answers to some of these questions by talking to people in schools and their local communities or examining publicly available data, including student survey findings, achievement test scores, graduation rates, student demographics, government budgets, legislation, or formal policy documents. Even if answers aren't easy to come by, raising these questions lets others know that you understand that all policies produce winners and losers. Maybe they'll begin to think about policy this way too.

You should definitely raise the questions above with the people elected (or hoping to be elected) to make policy decisions on your behalf. Research on successful policy-change efforts shows that advocates usually engage directly with policymakers, including school trustees and members of provincial government. You might send them letters or set up meetings. Some advocacy groups, such as SOS Alberta, provide letter templates you can use and/or a set of talking points. Some officials hold town hall meetings where you can raise issues of concern. These can be useful, but if there isn't an upcoming open forum you can attend another event where a trustee or MPP is and try to get their ear. They may brush you off at that time, but it may create an opportunity for you to follow up later. You might invite them to speak at an event you organize; it could be something on a small scale, like a conversation over coffee. When it comes to election time, be sure you vote for candidates who share your vision for public schools. You could also put a sign on your lawn or go a step further and volunteer on their campaigns to help them win.

Governments and school boards also have formal procedures to solicit and collect input on policy, including formal consultations and opportunities to speak to the board or its advisory committees. Events may take place in person, over the phone, or online. Participating may not be as simple as showing up, however. There will likely be a process for getting your name on a speakers or participants list, and there may be limits on how long you can talk. These details should be available on government and school district websites. Alternatively, some school boards have advisory committees you can join even if you are not a parent with a child enrolled in the district.

You can also ask critical questions about what's going in on your local schools. Are any of the privatization policies and practices I've discussed present or under consideration (e.g., fundraising, schools fees, specialized programs)? If so, who is benefitting from them? Who is losing? How can the policies and practices be challenged or improved? You may not be able to put a stop to them all at once, but there might be actions you can take to move in that direction.

Let's consider fees and fundraising. If you're a teacher, administrator, or school council member, you can stop asking parents to fundraise or pay fees. Not only does the practice exclude a lot of students and their families from activities in their own schools, but it also contributes to inequities between schools as well. If you want to take students on field trips, visit places you can walk to or invite community experts into your class instead. I bet many people in the community have skills or knowledge they'd be willing to share. Ask if they will donate their time. These guests could also include faculty and students from local universities, colleges or high schools. Inviting people normally outside of schools in may encourage them to pay closer attention to what's going on with public education while simultaneously broadening students' knowledge of their communities, not to mention subject content.

I know that many people see fundraising events as a great way to bring community members together, but couldn't the same objective be achieved through free events such as book talks, guest speakers, craft nights, or discussions about topics of interest? If you feel you have to fundraise or charge fees, make participating opt-in rather than opt-out. What might this look like? A school I know about hosts a pizza lunch that invites everyone to order pizza and to donate what they can to cover the costs. The money is submitted anonymously in an envelope separately from the pizza order forms. You might also recall from chapter 3 that some parents avoid joining school councils because they don't want to fundraise. To address this issue, school councils should consider setting up fundraising subcommittees so people not interested in fundraising might still join the council. If you are going to do this, however, be sure that people not on the subcommittee can participate in decisions about how to spend any fundraised dollars. Finally, school councils might also donate a portion of fundraised dollars to a central board fund for redistribution (or help establish one!).

Join the Public Dialogue

There are other ways you can challenge education privatization. You can write op-eds or letters to the editor, publish articles, write a blog, create a podcast, or comment on Twitter posts. You can share articles, books, documentaries, or data via social media and host a conversation with friends or family to discuss them. You could ask your school's parent council or principal to co-host with you. There may be university-based researchers who would be willing to present their work or facilitate a dialogue for free.

If you aren't comfortable acting alone, you might join an event organized by a group like the ones I described above. You could also join an existing organization. I joined East End Parents 4 Public Education just by sending a friend request through Facebook. Or, if you're up for it, you could even start your own group. You might reach out to leaders of another group to find out how they organized themselves. You could start by creating a social media account and inviting others with shared interests to join. If your local school has a parent or school council, you might attend a meeting and invite members to join. You could also ask them to post a notice in their newsletter, on their website, or via other communication they send out. If you're an educator or other school employee, check out what your union is up to.

Know What You're Up Against

Stopping education privatization is not going to be easy, and it's important to know this up front. There are many companies and individuals who stand to profit from greater private sector involvement in public education. The rapid turn to remote learning due to COVID-19 brought this potential to the fore as technology companies clamoured to grow their presence (and market share) in education.[16] Google, for example, offered "Teach from Anywhere," which promised to give "teachers and families the tools and tips they need to help keep students learning."[17] Microsoft created "Gaggle for Microsoft Teams," which provided "support for schools and districts by monitoring student communications for warning signs of crises" while using the software.[18] One projection saw the value of e-learning to be $325 billion by 2025 – and that was before the COVID-19 pandemic![19]

But it's not just about money. It's also about prevailing beliefs about the social world and how people should behave in it. In one of my studies I tried to understand why school fundraising policy has been so hard to change in Ontario despite decades of reform efforts and substantial evidence that the practice creates inequities in public education. Specifically, I wanted to know why opponents of the policy could not convince governments and other people to stop school fundraising. I looked at the arguments they made and how they mobilized them to elected officials and the public. They used all the strategies that successful policy actors had used in other campaigns, and yet opponents of school fundraising still could not achieve the outcome they hoped for. What I found was that their arguments just did not resonate with dominant ideas about society, success, and parenting.

As you know by this point in the book, one of those ideas is that the social world is best organized by market principles. Wendy Brown explains that this "political rationality" promotes competition and individualism and understands citizens as "rational economic actors" in all aspects of life.[20] In this view of society, people are expected to do everything they can to make themselves competitive in the marketplace. Individuals' successes and failures are attributed to their unwillingness or inability to compete. In this rationality, "good" parents do whatever they can to ensure their children are successful as well. School fundraising provides a way for parents to help make this happen if the money is used to buy materials and opportunities that will benefit their children. The idea of meritocracy is important here. Meritocracy is the belief that people who are successful have earned it through their hard work and good choices. Thus, they deserve their advantages and the ones they buy for their children. Meritocracy is a long-standing idea in Canada, and many of its citizens believe in it. It's a myth.

School fundraising makes even more sense when you remember that some governments have cut funding for public education while others have placed restrictions on how money must be spent. Some have done both. For parents who can afford to fundraise, notably the middle and upper classes, the practice helps ensure public schools will continue to reproduce their class advantages.

The fact that fundraising has a long history is also relevant. Lots of people have grown up with it without questioning its outcomes beyond the school. Add this history to the fact that it's touted as a great way to become involved in your kids' school and support your community, and it's no wonder that fundraising is viewed as both necessary and desirable. And, as I've tried to demonstrate throughout this book, policies promoting privatization have proliferated across Canada and around the world for decades. School fundraising is just one privatizing policy among many. My point here is that dominant ideas about how the world is best organized and how people should act in it influence policy-change efforts. Advocates can use strategies successful in other campaigns, some of which I've outlined above, but whether change happens or not depends on more than strategy alone.

Timing and serendipity also impact privatization. Unanticipated events can open "policy windows" that enable new policies and practices of all kinds to be adopted.[21] Advocates may have been pushing them for a long time, and when a window opens (i.e., an opportunity presents itself) they are ready with their policies in hand. Sometimes an emergency may be manufactured so that citizens will be more receptive to policy proposals. This was what John Snobelen, Ontario's education minister in 1995, hoped to do. He was infamously caught on tape saying that in order to generate support for the government's proposed education reforms "we need to invent a crisis."[22]

Of course, sometimes the crises that accelerate efforts to privatize education are real. Researcher Antoni Verger and his colleagues explain three reasons why catastrophes open the door for privatization.[23] First, crises provide external actors with greater presence, influence, and opportunities to test new ideas. Second, the sense of urgency experienced following a catastrophe means that transparent, democratic debates are less likely to take place. As a result, controversial policies can be introduced more easily. Finally, reforms adopted post-catastrophe tend to extend beyond the time and location of the event, thus impacting more people for longer periods of time.

The case of Hurricane Katrina in New Orleans, Louisiana, USA, is a prime example. Verger and colleagues explain that the need to quickly rebuild schools following the event made the public open to new and expanded school choice policies that many citizens had resisted prior to the hurricane. It was also harder for opponents to organize against the reforms since many of them were displaced by the storm. Local school districts took advantage of Louisiana's charter school laws, which allow individuals and groups outside public education systems to fund charter schools, and invited foundations to rebuild and operate charter schools in the city.[24] Eventually almost every public school was replaced with a privately managed charter school. Pro-market advocates were thus given the chance to test and their policy proposals, which they hoped they could later showcase across the country.[25] Unfortunately for them – and for the people of New Orleans – the promise that schools subject to fewer rules and greater competition would lead to better outcomes and schools for everyone failed to live up to the hype. Instead, schools became highly stratified, offering vastly different experiences for students.[26] What's more, the New Orleans Recovery School District has the lowest graduation rate in the state of Louisiana, and only 12 per cent of its students scored at the mastery level or above on state achievement tests in 2014 – nine years after the storm.[27]

I am writing in the midst of the COVID-19 pandemic, and its impacts on education privatization are unfolding. As I've already mentioned, the pandemic has elevated the role of technology in education through a turn to online learning long promoted by education-technology companies and resisted by many teacher unions and others opposed to education privatization. Some parents and caregivers are using commercial curricula and online programs to support homeschooling rather than sending their children back to school. Others are creating "pandemic pods" in which they, along with a few other families, form a bubble and hire a teacher to teach their children in their homes or a shared space. One media story reported an innovative take on the use of private funds for education:

a mother was considering removing her kids from their current private schools and enrolling them in the public system since both options were likely to use online learning. She explained, "That's basically like a 'free' curriculum and then, you know, we pay the additional (fees) to have somebody come in and coach them."[28]

In some sense, these are not "new" practices; homeschooling and private tutoring have long histories. However, more families are considering them in the face of fear for their kids' safety and/or the dissatisfaction with remote learning that they experienced in the spring of 2020. I understand these responses: it's a parent's or other primary caregiver's responsibility to look out for the best interests of their children. But it's the public's responsibility to look out for all kids' interests, and it's the job of critical policy researchers to investigate who benefits and who loses from policy.

While opponents of education privatization face formidable foes, their efforts are not futile. Resistance to education privatization is growing despite the influence of neoliberal ideology, private interests, philanthropic investments, and anticipated and unanticipated crises. Historian Diane Ravitch explains in her book *Slaying Goliath: The Passionate Resistance to Privatization and the Fight to Save America's Public Schools* that school choice policies in the United States are losing support because they have failed to deliver on their promises to increase student achievement and improve schooling for all.[29] As I detailed in in chapter 4, school choice policies based on the belief that market pressures will lead to higher academic achievement haven't lived up to these claims. And instead of waiting for policymakers to acknowledge education-privatization policies' failings, educators, students, parents, researchers, and other citizens are making those failings known.

Know that Public Education is Worth Fighting For

The fight for public education is worth it. Public schools are our best hope for achieving economic, social, and political justice since they are one of the few spaces where kids may get to know people very different from themselves and their families. If they are accessible to all, kids will have a better chance of developing respect for diverse beliefs, perspectives, and ways of living than they will if they attend schools segregated by race, class, language, religion, or other social categories. Public schooling is based on the idea that every child is of equal worth and deserves the same opportunity to realize all the benefits of education.

Education privatization undermines these beliefs. Policies that adopt private sector practices, such as creating education marketplaces through school choice policies and charging fees, exacerbate social inequalities by segregating students and creating unequal schools in terms of resources and opportunities. Kids cannot learn to value equality, inclusion, and fairness if they attend public schools that exclude some of their peers, if they themselves are shut out of opportunities, or if they observe some kids in public schools getting advantages not available to everyone. Instead they may learn that some people are more socially valued or deserving than others and that that's okay. Public schools become places where families get what they can for their own children and where historical and social inequalities are reproduced – at the public's (albeit dwindling) expense.

We need schools that reflect the public school ideal in order to achieve a socially just society. Such a society involves social, political, and economic justice.[30] More equal societies are healthier, have higher-quality social relationships, and have lower rates of social problems, including lower homicide rates, lower rates of imprisonment, and lower use of illegal drugs, than less equal societies.[31] Our governments need to fully fund public schools and elected officials need to pursue the public school ideal through policy. This will necessarily involve ongoing analysis of the impact of policies on different groups of students. When a policy is shown to create or reproduce inequity or otherwise threaten the public school ideal, it must be abandoned. Let's start by abandoning education privatization.

Appendix: Steps in Conducting Critical Policy Research

In a 2014 grant application, I proposed to study how an advocacy group in Ontario attempted to influence policies related to school fundraising and wait times for special education testing. I explained in my proposal that my project would be different from most research on interest groups in education. Not only would it focus on two long-term and low-profile campaigns of a single group in Canada, it would be based on critical assumptions about policy rather than more common rational understandings. I defined policy as a struggle over meaning and set out to examine how the group understood fundraising and special education testing in Ontario and the strategies they used to persuade the Ontario government to see the issues in the ways they did.

I proposed to use a multiple case study approach and said I'd work with two graduate students to study two of the group's campaigns, one successful (fundraising) and one not-yet- successful (reduction of wait times for special education testing). We'd collect data from interviews with five of the group's members, documents the group produced about each policy issue, as well as media reports, government policy texts, and transcripts from submissions to Ontario's legislature. I said we'd also interview two journalists who reported on the group's efforts in these campaigns, two government officials who developed the fundraising policy, two government officials who work in the area of special education, and four activists also trying to influence these policies. I said we'd use rhetorical analysis to identify how the group constructed its arguments to persuade audiences to accept its meanings of the two policies and support their preferred courses of action. I proposed that the project would take two years.

Well, things didn't go quite as planned. For one thing, as soon as we started collecting and reading media articles about the group's campaigns we realized that while we viewed the practice of schools charging parents fees as a kind of fundraising, neither the group nor the government agreed. They saw the issues as separate, and the group advocated for distinct policies to address school fees and fundraising. Also, rereading my notes from an interview with a group member in a previous study, I realized they hadn't pointed to their efforts to get a fundraising policy in place as a success, but rather it was their campaign to have the government eliminate fees for learning materials that was successful. Indeed, the government had introduced a fees policy that seemed to have had an impact on the kinds of fees charged by schools. When it came to fundraising, however, the practice continued to grow in spite of new fundraising guidelines introduced by the government. Now we had three campaigns to consider, not two, and we had to rethink what we meant by success. Could the new fundraising guidelines be considered successful if the practice hadn't changed? We decided it couldn't; so what I proposed to study as a successful campaign became another not-yet-successful one in our project.

Another difference between what I proposed and what actually happened relates to the data we collected. Yes, we examined the texts I proposed we would, but we didn't end up conducting any interviews. This change was largely due to our ability to answer our research questions without needing the interview data. Interviews take a lot of time to conduct and transcribe, and we didn't think we needed to do this extra work. A bigger issue was emerging though. It was partly theoretical and partly methodological. The more we read about the issues, the more it was clear that many individuals and groups were lobbying the government to address the school fees, fundraising, and special education wait times, not just the group we were studying. In fact, many were making the same arguments. While we would be able to identify their persuasive strategies, would we be able to claim that any official policy changes were a direct result of the actions of the group we were studying? I realized I needed a new theory of policy change that could help me think about how one group's efforts fit with those of other policy actors. I found one, argumentative discourse theory, and conducted another small study using some of our data and findings to see what I could learn about policy advocacy and change using this new way to think about these processes.

Even though the study didn't unfold as planned, I learned a lot. We were able to explain why the arguments our group – and others – made were influential in one campaign but not others, and we were able to create new knowledge about education-policy advocacy in Ontario. I also learned to let go of the idea that it is possible to figure out exactly who or what influences policy and to live with the discomfort I felt about this new knowledge. Importantly, I continued to work with argumentative discourse theory in future projects.

In this appendix I try to give you a sense of what's involved in doing critical policy analysis. I'm hoping this brief discussion will provide you with a general understanding of how the critical scholars referenced in this book, including me, conduct their work. If you are interested in conducting your own critical policy research, I hope the steps I discuss are useful as you develop and undertake your work. Note that while I present the steps sequentially, they don't neatly follow one after the other. If you are planning and undertaking research you may find yourself moving back and forth between some steps or combining others. Indeed, even in writing them out I've had a hard time determining where one step ends and another begins. I can say, however, that any critical policy study I've conducted has involved all of them at some point. My intention here is to provide an introduction to conducting critical policy research rather than a comprehensive "how-to" guide. Throughout the discussion I refer to resources new and aspiring policy scholars might find useful based on my own experiences.

Step 1: Identify a Policy Topic

First, you need to select a policy to study. An idea for what to study can come from anywhere – personal experience, media reports, a new government policy, existing research, a podcast, conversations with colleagues or friends, or someplace else. For example, I chose the topic of my doctoral research, character education, based on my teaching experiences and my hope that my young son would become one of the "good guys." I wanted to know what I could do to foster empathy within him as he grew, and I wondered what role, if any, schools could play. An interview with a teacher I conducted for my qualitative research class about "how schools teach empathy" reminded me about character education, an area of curriculum I knew but had forgotten. Many schools adopt formal character education programs that aim to teach values, including empathy. As I read about these initiatives in academic articles and teaching resources I learned they are often based on the belief that there are universal values that all cultures and religions share. Recalling my own experiences teaching values to students in Mexico, Canada, and the United States, I felt that class, religious, linguistic, nationality and other differences between me and my students *had* mattered, contrary to the claims of many character education advocates I had read. I wondered about the consequences of ignoring differences between how my students and I understood what it meant to show respect or responsibility. My search for a dissertation topic also coincided with a provincial election, and the Liberal Party leader at that time, Dalton McGuinty, was promising to mandate character education in all Ontario public schools if he was elected. For all these reasons (i.e., personal interest, professional experiences, policy commitment) I chose to focus my research on character education.

Once you find a topic that interests you, it's a good idea to then review what is already known and written about it. This usually involves reading existing research, including academic journals and books. This literature will not only tell you what scholars know about your area of interest but it will also help you figure out what is not known. In addition, you can learn how and where the topic has been studied. You may find that a lot has been written about it but not necessarily from a policy perspective or in a particular time or space. In addition to academic sources, you might review media sources, professional journals, and reports written by governments and non-government organizations. This literature can give you a sense of how the issue is understood by people in different social locations and their concerns. If possible, talk to people who are familiar with the topic so you can glean further understanding of various perspectives on and dimensions of the issue.

After you've identified a topic that really engages you, you need to figure out if and how you might study it from a policy perspective. This is one moment when debates over the meaning of policy become very important. How you define policy will impact how you design your study. If you define policy as a text or decision of government, for example, then you will need an official text or evidence of a decision (e.g., transcripts of government debates) for you to do the study. Alternatively, if you define policy as an ongoing social practice then you will need to determine if you can study what people do in their everyday activities in relation to your area of interest. Adopting a policy-as-discourse understanding requires different approaches. I find that most topics can be studied through a policy lens. If it is going to be a critically oriented study, you will, of course, need to pay attention to how the policy challenges and/or perpetuates social inequalities.

In my work I adopt a multifaceted definition of policy based on Bowe, Ball, and Gold's policy cycle. As I explained in chapter 2, the policy cycle recognizes three interrelated arenas of action: the context of influence; the context of text production; and the context of practice. In my various projects I tend to examine one of these contexts closely and consider the other two when it makes sense to do so. For example, in one study of Ontario's school fundraising I examined various actors' advocacy for and against the practice in the policy's *context of influence*.[1] In particular, I wanted to understand why the practice is so common and why it is so hard to change. To answer this question I examined a wide range of data sources in the context of text production, including media articles, parliamentary debates, political party platform documents, government texts, advocacy organizations' websites and print materials, and research reports in order to figure out advocates' and opponents' arguments for and against fundraising. I considered their arguments in relation to Ontario's socio-historical context to help me understand why some arguments resonated widely while others did not. I concluded that in a context that advocates individualism, privatization, and reduced government spending on public services, giving private money to public schools through fundraising to provide their children with opportunities to enhance their chance of success in a competitive and unpredictable world makes sense to a lot of parents. As I also explained in chapter 2, government and school district policies that endorse school fundraising alongside fundraising practices create unequal access to opportunities in public schools and recreate unequal social relations that exist outside them.

This study, like any study that examines a policy's context of influence, taught me who was involved in the policy debate as well as their arguments and rhetorical strategies. I learned about the history of the practice and how it had evolved over time in response to changing political, cultural, and economic discourses and circumstances. Of course, this study couldn't tell me everything about fundraising in Ontario. It couldn't tell me how fundraising takes place in schools or why the practice looks different in different places, for example. Answering these kinds of questions requires a focus on fundraising policy's *context of practice* since studies in this context pay close attention to what people think, believe, and do. Thus, in another study that began in the context of practice of the Toronto District School Board's (TDSB) fundraising policy, I investigated parents', principals', and school council members' fundraising work.[2] In interviews I asked study participants to tell me exactly what they did when running fundraising initiatives and how they make decisions about what to do. As they talked, I learned about various documents in the context of text production that informed their work in schools.

My analysis of these texts and the interview transcripts helped me see that TDSB parents' fundraising practices are not only organized by fundraising, parent involvement, and school council policies of the TDSB and Ontario Ministry of Education; their local experiences are also impacted by the decisions and activities of their children's principal and parent members of the school council, not to mention the financial resources of the school's community. These findings help explain why variations in fundraising exist between schools, an explanation I wasn't able to glean from my examination of fundraising-policy advocacy. This study also revealed the incredible amount of free labour that some parents contribute, which not only provides their children and others in their schools with access to resources and opportunities but also yields financial benefits to for-profit businesses. If you are interested in understanding what people actually do "on the ground"; how they make meaning of government, district, or other policies; and the consequences of their actions, then investigating a policy's context of practice would probably be a good choice.

If, however, you are interested in what policy texts say, the discourses they contain and mobilize, how they relate to one another or have changed over time, or their possible implications, you might want to focus on a policy's *context of text production*. This is what Michelle Milani and I did in an examination of a government document as part of a larger critical analysis of school fundraising in Ontario.[3] We analysed the content of Ontario's *Fundraising Guideline* to determine if and how the official policy addressed the democratic values of equity, inclusion, participatory decision-making processes, and critical mindedness. We noted that the *Fundraising Guideline* says that schools should "consider the purposes and principles of public education, including diversity, accessibility, and inclusivity" when engaging in fundraising and that fundraising activities should align with the province's Equity and Inclusive Education Strategy.[4] Thus, while the *Fundraising Guideline* could be said to promote the critical democratic values of equity and inclusion, the absence of consequences for schools that don't comply with its expectations suggests its function is primarily symbolic. The findings of our study helped us identify the policy's inconsistencies and suggested how they could be exploited by people looking to curb school fundraising. To see how people actually interpret the *Guideline*, however, would require examining what people do in the context of practice.

I hope it's clear from these examples how a focus on one policy context allows you as a researcher to understand aspects of a particular policy that a focus on another context would not. At the same time, as I said above, even when my research focuses on one context, I can't help but consider the other contexts: if I focus on the context of practice, I might be interested in not only what people do, but also why they do what they do. Understanding the *why* might lead to me look at governing or instructive texts and/or the historical and social conditions, including discourses, impacting people's actions. Also, remember that critical policy theorists insist that a policy's socio-historical context be taken into account; doing so normally requires considering the context of influence.

Step 2: Develop a Research Question

Once you have narrowed your focus for the study you will need to specify your research questions to guide the study. This step is often more difficult than it might seem. Sometimes I find it hard to articulate what it is I want to know, and often I'm interested in learning much more than a single project can address. Sometimes the questions I want answered cannot be answered through research due to various practical, ethical, financial, or other constraints.

I'm going to again use Bowe et al.'s policy cycle as a way to show various kinds of questions you might pose about your policy topic. You might also check out the lists provided by Bob Lingard and Fazal Rizvi in their book, *Globalizing Educational Policy*, and by Lesley Vidovich for even more possibilities.[5] Let's say I am interested in policy texts. I might ask, What texts address this policy? Who produced them? What do they say? How do the texts construct the policy issue and the people involved in it? What discourses are present in the texts? For example, in my study of a school board's character education policy, *Character Matters!*, I posed the following questions:

1 What is the approach to character education advocated by *Character Matters!*?
2 How is the argument for this approach constructed in *Character Matters!*?[6]

If, on the other hand, I wanted to understand influences on policy texts and practices, I would focus on the policy's context of influence and ask questions such as, Why was this policy created? Who advocated for this policy? Why? Did anyone oppose it? Why? How do different people understand the meaning of the policy? How do they try to convince others to see it as they do? Whose voices are absent, and whose dominate? What are the historical and social discourses that support this policy? In my study of public funding of private schools in two Canadian provinces I asked the following research questions (among others):

1 What are the story lines in debates over public funding of private schools in Alberta and Ontario and who are the actors that mobilized them?
2 How have shifting cultural, economic and political contexts at multiple scales influenced struggles over the meaning of public funding of private schools in each province?

Answering these two questions didn't tell me anything about how people in private schools understand government decisions about whether or not to fund private schools or, in those provinces that do, how people in private schools spend the public dollars. To understand these processes my questions would need to focus on how people make sense of policy texts in local sites and policy actors' practices. I might also be interested in the roles of various actors or the impact of their practices. Of course, since all of my research is critically oriented, I always consider what the answers to my research questions tell me about the ways in which the policy I'm studying (whether it be its related texts, practices, or influences) challenges or reproduces social inequalities. I also ask, Who benefits from this policy and who loses?

Step 3: Consider Engaging Multiple Theories

Since you are committed to understanding how policies advantage some groups while disadvantaging others, you might consider engaging other critical theories in your study to help you think through how this happens. Many researchers use critical policy theories in combination with other theoretical frameworks in their studies to help them hone in on particular areas of interest. While there are numerous possible combinations, I discuss a few examples to demonstrate benefits of using multiple theories in a single study.

Naomi Nichols and Alison Griffith use institutional ethnography to ground their study of how principals, teachers, and parents actualize accountability policies through their talk and action.[7] Institutional ethnography is a good fit for critically oriented policy studies because its emphasis on texts helps show how policy documents in combination with other texts organize people's lives in ways that reproduce social inequalities. Lois Andre-Becheley's study of how parents negotiate school choice policies in a US school district combines institutional ethnography with critical race theory (CRT) to explain how race operates in this process.[8] Using CRT makes race more "visible" to policy researchers.[9] In Andre-Becheley's study, CRT helped reveal how the district's school choice policies and its historical and legal contexts, including court-ordered desegregation, created advantages for white students.

In my critical policy study of public funding of private schools, I used Martaan Hajer's argumentative discourse theory to explain how policy actors and their arguments shift in response to changing cultural, economic, and political contexts at multiple scales.[10] This theory, with its emphasis on identifying members of groups who mobilize the same arguments in struggles over policy even though they don't know each other, helped me identify people involved in advocacy in ways and in places that I may have otherwise overlooked. It also helped me understand how actors who don't know each other are connected through time and space as they struggle to change or maintain policies that create different patterns of advantage.

These three examples are meant to show you that using one or more theories to think with as you conduct your critically oriented research policy research can produce new understandings that might not have otherwise surfaced. Other theories used by policy scholars in their critical policy research include critical discourse analysis,[11] Actor Network Theory,[12] critical feminist theory,[13] critical democracy,[14] queer theory,[15] and many more.

Step 4: Design Your Study

You then need to design your study. This step involves choosing the methodology you will use. Ideally, the research design you select is the one that will best enable you to answer your research questions. Sometimes the best design may not be feasible given the practical realities of doing research (e.g., limited time and money, access to data sources), so you need to be prepared to make adjustments as needed. Critical policy analysts use a wide range of methodologies and methods in their work. A methodology is the overall approach to your study, whereas methods are the specific tools you use to collect data and answer your research questions.[16] Critical policy analysts often, although not always, use qualitative approaches to research.[17] Your research questions and the theories grounding your study will inform your methodology and methods.

Indeed, in critical-oriented policy research, theory and methodology are interconnected.[18] If you understand policy as discourse, for example, and you are interested in understanding the impact of policy discourses, you will likely use critical discourse analysis as both a theory and methodology. Similarly, institutional ethnography is both a theory of the social world and an approach to enquiry. Researchers who draw on CRT might collect counterstories as a method as part of their effort to learn about the experiences of racialized people and to bring these individuals' stories to light.[19] The authors in Michelle D. Young and Sarah Diem's edited book, *Critical Approaches to Education Policy Analysis: Moving Beyond Tradition*, offer detailed discussions of the relationship between the theories and methodologies they use in the critical policy research studies presented in their chapters. This book is a great resource for people who want to know more about how theory informs methodological choices in critical policy research.

You will need to make decisions about what data will help you answer your research questions, how to collect that data, and how to analyse them once you've got them. Sometimes the best data sources for your project are obvious. For example, if you want to know how children feel about homework the best source of this information are kids themselves. To collect information about their feelings you might interview them, ask them to fill out a questionnaire, have them draw a picture of themselves doing homework, or use some other method. There are many possible ways to collect data; I can't review them all here. You should read books specifically about research methods, read research to find out how others have collected data, and talk to more experienced researchers. The same is true for deciding how you will make sense of the data you collect in ways that help you answer your research questions (this process is called data analysis). The methods of data collection and analysis you choose will depend in part on the assumptions about the social world that underlie your project and the purposes of your research. If you want to be able to make predictions about what happens to Y if something happens to X, for example, then you will need to use statistical methods that are supposed to be able to show these kinds of relationships. The statistical tests you choose will determine how many participants you need in your study and how to figure out who they should be.

Sometimes the most obvious or ideal data sources are not possible to access for ethical or practical (e.g., time, money) reasons, so you will have to settle for the second- or even third-best sources. And there are times when you don't have to collect data yourself; you can look at other people's research findings or data. Findings might be published in reports or articles, and data collected by others can sometimes be obtained through requests to the researcher(s) or on institutional repositories. I refer to other researchers' findings a lot in this book. There is simply no way – or need – for me to conduct original research on every policy topic related to privatization in Canada. Among other questions, when reading others' research I typically ask, What does this study's findings tell me about if/how the policy challenges or reproduces social inequalities? What does it tell me about who benefits and who loses from this policy?

If your study involves collecting data from people and you are affiliated with a university, you will have to seek approval to carry out your research from your institution's ethics-review committee. Once approved, depending on where you want to collect data you may need to apply for ethics approval from another committee. School boards, for example, will often have their own review processes, and they may not even look at your application until you get approval from your institution. If you aren't affiliated with a university but want to get assurance that your study meets ethical standards, you may seek approval from some community-based centres that have been set up for this purpose.

Now let's look at a specific example. Earlier in this appendix, I told you about a critical policy study I conducted that was based on Hajer's argumentative discourse theory. The theory states that policies change when actors successfully change their dominant meanings. I wanted to find out who was involved in debates over public funding of private schools, the arguments they mobilized, and why one perspective prevailed in one province but not another. To answer these questions, I planned to use methodology proposed by Hajer: argumentative discourse analysis (ADA). ADA involves a number of steps. It suggests potential data sources and questions to ask of the data during the analysis. However, I was interested in understanding how debates unfolded in three provinces over time. I couldn't find any studies where ADA was used to examine multiple sites over decades, and I needed a way to think about the comparative aspects of my project. So I turned to Barlett and Vavrus's comparative case study approach.[20]

These authors suggest that individual sites (i.e., cases) of a phenomenon can be compared in at least three ways. One way is to compare similar cases at the same level or scale. You might, for example, compare three grade 10 math classes in a single school, four provincial policies on standardized testing, or two countries' graduation requirements. A second way to compare is to examine international, national, provincial, and local influences on a particular case. This could involve looking at how teacher education at a particular university is impacted by what is going on outside the Faculty of Education itself (e.g., provincial funding decisions, national policies on job mobility, growing numbers of international students attending local public schools). A third way to study the phenomenon is to look at how it has changed over time.

I decided to combine the comparative case study approach with ADA to answer my research questions. My cases included debates over public funding of private schools in Ontario and Alberta. I focused on each case separately to begin. My research assistants and I determined who were the actors in the debate; what they argued; influences on their arguments; and if, how, and why the people and arguments changed over time. Data sources included media articles, interviews with actors involved in the debates, transcripts from parliamentary meetings, advocacy organizations' publications, and others' research. We read each data source, highlighted arguments made for and against the policy, grouped similar arguments in categories, and identified the actors that made each argument. Once the cases were complete, we compared them to figure out similarities and differences between what took place in each of the two provinces and why.

Step 5: Carry Out Your Study

As I described in this appendix's opening narrative, research often doesn't go as planned. As you set out to collect your data you may face unanticipated challenges. What if no one volunteers to participate in your study? What if you can't find the documents you planned to analyse? What if school boards won't let you into their schools due to labour action or even a pandemic? There's no way I can cover all the possible challenges that might arise. You really need to be prepared to change your plans. You might have to look to a different data source, find a new recruitment strategy, or change your data collection plan.

Even when you don't face challenges getting your data, other questions arise. Let me return to my study about debates of public funding of private schools to give you an example. My first step was to collect media articles that reported details about the debates. Easier said than done. Which newspapers should I look at? Should I focus only on print editions or include online ones as well? My team and I decided that we would pick two newspapers for each site; one would be national in focus and the other would be local. We then needed to figure out the search terms we would use to find the articles; terms that were too broad yielded hundreds of articles, while terms that were too narrow produced only a few hits. We eventually decided to collect articles centred around key incidents over a span of thirty-five years. This helped make our searches more manageable, but we worried we were missing advocacy efforts that were taking place but not captured by journalists.

When we focused on debate over the introduction of a tax credit for parents who send their children to private schools in Ontario in 2001, we were surprised at how few articles we had collected reported on the issue. I recalled reading transcripts of parliamentary committee meetings where people could present their views on the tax credit and knew that we were missing a lot of actors. I decided to analyse those transcripts using the strategy we used for the media articles. Doing so showed me that we were definitely failing to identify some actors; this was a problem because we were trying to capture a wide range of actors participating in the debates. At the same time, the number of codes and length of time it took to review the documents were substantial. We wondered if we should collect more data each case. In the end we decided to limit our data to the two newspapers and interviews with select policy actors, document our rationale, and live with the knowledge that our study – like all studies – would have its limitations due to the choices we made in the process.

I could say a lot more about designing and carrying out a critical policy study, but I could never cover every possible design or challenge. What I've tried to do in this section is give you an overview of what's involved in doing research and highlight some key issues and decisions you will need to make along the way. Many of my points are relevant to any research project, not just a critically oriented policy study. As I've tried to emphasize, what makes critical policy studies "critical" are their main purposes: to expose how power circulates throughout policy processes; to reveal policy winners and losers; to discover the impact of policy on patterns of social inequality; and to identify possibilities for resistance and change.

Notes

1. Educational Privatization and Public Education in Canada

1　While I use the term "parent" throughout the book, I recognize other caregivers may assume responsibilities for children as well.
2　Jennifer Wallner, *Learning to School: Federalism and Public Schooling in Canada* (Toronto: University of Toronto Press, 2014), 4, http://ebookcentral .proquest.com/lib/york/detail.action?docID=3292645.
3　Wallner, *Learning to School*, 76–80.
4　Statistics Canada, "Number and Proportion of Students in Elementary and Secondary Schools, by School Type, Canada, Provinces and Territories, 2017/2018," 24 October 2019, https://www150.statcan.gc.ca/n1 /daily-quotidien/191024/t001b-eng.htm.
5　Scott Davies and Janice Aurini, "Exploring School Choice in Canada: Who Chooses What and Why?" *Canadian Public Policy / Analyse de politiques* 37, no. 4 (2011): 473.
6　Doug Hart and Arlo Kempf, *Public Attitudes toward Education in Ontario: The 20th OISE Survey of Educational Issues 2018* (Toronto: Ontario Institute for Studies in Education, 2018), 9, https://www.oise.utoronto.ca/oise /News/2018/2018_OISE_Survey_of_Educational_Issues.html.
7　Ministry of Education, *2019 Education Stakeholder Surveys Summary Report* (Edmonton: Government of Alberta, December 2019), 4, https://open .alberta.ca/publications/9781460146101.
8　Mario Canseco, "Class Sizes, Teacher Shortage Worry Parents in British Columbia," Research Co., 5 June 2019, https://researchco.ca/2019/06 /05/strong-words-in-the-staffroom-the-accusations-fly/.
9　Michael Mindzak, "What Happened to Charter Schools in Canada?" *Equity & Excellence in Education* 48, no. 1 (2 January 2015): 114, https:// doi.org/10.1080/10665684.2015.991162.

10 Sue Saltmarsh, "Michel de Certeau, Everyday Life and Policy Cultures: The Case of Parent Engagement in Education Policy," *Critical Studies in Education* 56, no. 1 (2 January 2015): 43, https://doi.org/10.1080/17508487 .2015.961166. Sue Winton, "Challenging Fundraising, Challenging Inequity: Contextual Constraints on Advocacy Groups' Policy Influence," *Critical Studies in Education* 59, no. 1 (2 January 2018): 65, https://doi.org /10.1080/17508487.2016.1176062.

11 Statistics Canada, "Number and Proportion of Students in Elementary and Secondary Schools, by School Type, Canada, Provinces and Territories, 2016/2017," Government of Canada, 2 November 2018, https:// www150.statcan.gc.ca/n1/daily-quotidien/181102/dq181102c-eng. htm.

12 Lynn Bosetti, Deani Van Pelt, and Derek J. Allison, "The Changing Landscape of School Choice in Canada: From Pluralism to Parental Preference?" *Education Policy Analysis Archives* 25, no. 38 (April 2017): 8.

13 Bosetti, Van Pelt, and Allison, "The Changing Landscape," 17–18.

14 Janice Aurini and Scott Davies, "Choice without Markets: Homeschooling in the Context of Private Education," *British Journal of Sociology of Education* 26, no. 4 (1 January 2005): 469, https://doi.org/10.1080 /01425690500199834; Bosetti, Van Pelt, and Alison, "The Changing Landscape," 19–20.

15 Christopher Lubienski, "School Choice and Privatization in Education: An Alternative Analytical Framework," *Journal for Critical Education Policy Studies* 4, no. 1 (2006): 13, http://www.jceps.com/archives/511; Canadian Centre for Policy Alternatives, *Health Care, Limited* (Ottawa: Canadian Centre for Policy Alternatives, 2000), 8, https://www .policyalternatives.ca/publications/reports/health-care-limited.

16 Emily Winchip, Howard Stevenson, and Alison Milner, "Measuring Privatisation in Education: Methodological Challenges and Possibilities," *Educational Review* 71, no. 1 (2 January 2019): 83, https://doi.org/10.1080 /00131911.2019.1524197.

17 Stephen J. Ball and Deborah Youdell, *Hidden Privatisation in Public Education* (Education International Brussels, 2007), 9–10.

18 Heather-jane Robertson, "The Many Faces of Privatization," *Our Schools, Our Selves* (Summer 2005): 49.

19 Ball and Youdell, 23; Christopher Lubienski, "Sector Distinctions and the Privatization of Public Education Policymaking," *Theory and Research in Education* 14, no. 2 (1 July 2016): 200, https://doi.org/10.1177 /1477878516635332.

20 Ball and Youdell, "Sector Distinctions," 18–23.

21 Alison I. Griffith and Dorothy E. Smith, "Introduction," in *Under New Public Management: Institutional Ethnographies of Changing Front-Line Work*, ed. Alison I. Griffith and Dorothy E. Smith (Toronto: University of Toronto Press, 2014), 5.

22 Gary Anderson and Michael Cohen, "Redesigning the Identities of Teachers and Leaders: A Framework for Studying New Professionalism and Educator Resistance," *Education Policy Analysis Archives* 23 (10 September 2015): 5–6, https://doi.org/10.14507/epaa.v23.2086; Goli M. Rezai-Rashti and Allison Segeren, "The Game of Accountability: Perspectives of Urban School Leaders on Standardized Testing in Ontario and British Columbia, Canada," *International Journal of Leadership in Education* (15 November 2020): 9–14, https://doi.org/10.1080/13603124.2020.1808711; Paul Bocking, *Public Education, Neoliberalism, and Teachers: New York, Mexico City, Toronto* (Toronto: University of Toronto Press, 2020), 203, http://ebookcentral.proquest.com/lib/york/detail.action?docID=6154665.

23 Bocking, *Public Education*, 203.

24 York Region District School Board, "School Application – Registration," Bill Crothers Secondary School, 2019, http://www.yrdsb.ca/schools/billcrothers.ss/info/Pages/School-Registration.aspx.

25 Gita Steiner-Khamsi, "The Global Education Industry," FreshEd with Will Brehm, accessed 6 August 2020, http://www.freshedpodcast.com/gitasteinerkhamsi/.

26 Antoni Verger, Clara Fontdevila, and Adrián Zancajo, *The Privatization of Education: A Political Economy of Global Education Reform* (New York: Teachers College Press, 2016): 11.

27 Verger, Fontdevila, and Zancajo, *The Privatization of Education*, 69.

28 Verger, Fontdevila, and Zancajo, 69.

29 Adam Davidson-Harden and Suzanne Majhanovich, "Privatisation of Education in Canada: A Survey of Trends," *International Review of Education / Internationale Zeitschrift Für Erziehungswissenschaft / Revue internationale de l'éducation* 50, nos. 3/4 (2004): 271–5.

30 For example, see Jamie Brownlee, *Academia, Inc.: How Corporatization Is Transforming Canadian Universities* (Halifax: Fernwood Publishing, 2015), https://fernwoodpublishing.ca/book/academia-inc; Peter P. Grimmett, "Neoliberalism as a Prevailing Force on the Conditions of Teacher Education in Canada," *Alberta Journal of Educational Research* 64, no. 4 (2018): 346–63; Marjorie Johnstone and Eunjung Lee, "Canada and the Global Rush for International Students: Reifying a Neo-Imperial Order of Western Dominance in the Knowledge Economy Era," *Critical Sociology* 43, nos. 7–8 (1 November 2017): 1063–78, https://doi.org/10.1177

/0896920516654554; Dale M. McCartney and Amy Scott Metcalfe, "Corporatization of Higher Education through Internationalization: The Emergence of Pathway Colleges in Canada," *Tertiary Education and Management* 24, no. 3 (1 September 2018): 206–20, https://doi.org/10.1080 /13583883.2018.1439997.

31 Catherine Gidney, *Captive Audience: How Corporations Invaded Our Schools* (Toronto: Between the Lines, 2019).

32 Gidney, *Captive Audience*, 32.

33 Ann Porter, "Neo-Conservatism, Neo-Liberalism and Canadian Social Policy: Challenges for Feminism," *Canadian Woman Studies* 29, no. 3 (2012): 20; Bryan M. Evans and Charles W. Smith, "Introduction: Transforming Provincial Politics: The Political Economy of Canada's Provinces and Territories in a Neoliberal Era," in *Transforming Provincial Politics: The Political Economy of Canada's Provinces and Territories in the Neoliberal Era*, ed. Bryan M. Evans and Charles W. Smith (Toronto: University of Toronto Press, 2015), 5.

34 Wendy Larner, "Neo-Liberalism: Policy, Ideology, Governmentality," *Studies in Political Economy* 63 (2000): 7.

35 Raewyn Connell, "The Neoliberal Cascade and Education: An Essay on the Market Agenda and Its Consequences," *Critical Studies in Education* 54, no. 2 (2013): 100.

36 A.M. Viens, "Neo-Liberalism, Austerity and the Political Determinants of Health," *Health Care Analysis* 27, no. 3 (2019): 149, https://doi.org /10.1007/s10728-019-00377-7.

37 Naomi Nichols and Alison I. Griffith, "Talk, Texts, and Educational Action: An Institutional Ethnography of Policy in Practice," *Cambridge Journal of Education* 39, no. 2 (1 June 2009): 241–55, https://doi.org /10.1080/03057640902902286.

38 Antonio Olmedo and Andrew Wilkins, "Governing through Parents: A Genealogical Enquiry of Education Policy and the Construction of Neoliberal Subjectivities in England," *Discourse: Studies in the Cultural Politics of Education* 38, no. 4 (4 July 2017): 574, https://doi.org/10.1080/01596306 .2015.1130026; Samantha Hedges et al., "Private Actors and Public Goods: A Comparative Case Study of Funding and Public Governance in K–12 Education in 3 Global Cities," *Journal of Educational Administration and History* 52, no. 1 (2 January 2020): 104, https://doi.org/10.1080/00220620.2019 .1685474.

39 Wendy Brown, *In the Ruins of Neoliberalism: The Rise of Antidemocratic Politics in the West* (New York: Columbia University Press, 2019), 29.

40 Brown, *Ruins of Neoliberalism*, 31.
41 Brown, 33.
42 Brown, 38–9.
43 Porter, "Neo-Conservatism," 20.
44 Michael W. Apple, "Understanding and Interrupting Neoliberalism and Neoconservatism in Education," *Pedagogies: An International Journal* 1, no. 1 (2006): 22, https://doi.org/10.1207/s15544818ped0101_4.
45 Apple, "Understanding," 22–3.
46 Laura Elizabeth Pinto, "Race and Fear of the 'Other' in Common Sense Revolution Reforms," *Critical Education* 4, no. 2 (15 February 2013), https://doi.org/10.14288/ce.v4i2.182344.
47 See for example Chris Ross Arthur, "The Ethics of Entrepreneurship and Financial Literacy Education: A Security and Freedom for the Other" (Toronto: York University, 2016), https://yorkspace.library.yorku.ca/xmlui/handle/10315/32265; Sue Winton, "The Appeal(s) of Character Education in Threatening Times: Caring and Critical Democratic Responses," *Comparative Education* 44, no. 3 (2008): 305–16; Sue Winton and Stephanie Tuters, "Constructing Bullying in Ontario, Canada: A Critical Policy Analysis," *Educational Studies* 41, nos. 1–2 (15 March 2015): 122–42, https://doi.org/10.1080/03055698.2014.955737.
48 Stephen J. Ball, "Big Policies/Small World: An Introduction to International Perspectives in Education Policy," *Comparative Education* 34, no. 2 (1998): 123–4.
49 Claudia Milena Diaz Rios, "Foreign Prescriptions and Domestic Interests: A Comparison of Education Reform in Argentina and Chile," *Journal of Comparative Policy Analysis: Research and Practice* 20, no. 2 (15 March 2018): 193–208, https://doi.org/10.1080/13876988.2016.1239321.
50 Prachi Srivastava, "Questioning the Global Scaling up of Low-Fee Private Schooling: The Nexus between Business, Philanthropy, and PPPs," in *World Yearbook of Education 2016: The Global Education Industry*, ed. Antoni Verger, Christopher Lubienski, and Gita Steiner-Khamsi (New York: Routledge, 2016), 248–63.
51 Craig Skerritt and Maija Salokangas, "Patterns and Paths towards Privatisation in Ireland," *Journal of Educational Administration and History* 52, no. 1 (2020): 84–99, https://doi.org/10.1080/00220620.2019.1689104.
52 Jessica Gerrard and Rosie Barron, "Cleaning Public Education: The Privatisation of School Maintenance Work," *Journal of Educational Administration*

and History 52, no. 1 (2 January 2020): 9–21, https://doi.org/10.1080 /00220620.2019.1689102.

53 Nicole Mockler et al., "Explaining Publicness: A Typology for Understanding the Provision of Schooling in Contemporary Times," in *Privatisation and Commercialisation in Public Education: How the Public Nature of Schooling Is Changing*, ed. Anna Hogan and Greg Thompson (London: Routledge, 2020), 201.

54 Jonathan Young, Benjamin Levin, and Dawn Wallin, *Understanding Canadian Schools: An Introduction to Educational Administration* (Toronto: Nelson Education, 2006), 12.

55 Wendy Poole and Gerald Fallon, "The Emerging Fourth Tier in K–12 Education Finance in British Columbia, Canada: Increasing Privatisation and Implications for Social Justice," *Globalisation, Societies and Education* 13, no. 3 (2015): 340.

56 Rovell Patrick Solomon and John P. Portelli, "Introduction," in *The Erosion of Democracy in Education: Critique to Possibilities*, ed. Rovell Patrick Solomon and John P. Portelli (Calgary: Detselig Enterprises, 2001), 19; D. Stewart, "Purposes of Public Education: Philosophical Reflections," *Education Canada* 45, no. 1 (2005): 5; Jon Young, "Reflecting Today, Creating Tomorrow: The Dual Role of Public Education," *Education Canada* 44, no. 4 (2004): 15.

57 Bob Lingard, "Policy Borrowing, Policy Learning: Testing Times in Australian Schooling," *Critical Studies in Education* 51, no. 2 (2010): 136.

58 Jessica Gerrard, "Public Education in Neoliberal Times: Memory and Desire," *Journal of Education Policy* 30, no. 6 (2 November 2015): 866, https://doi.org/10.1080/02680939.2015.1044568.

59 Paul Axelrod, *The Promise of Schooling: Education in Canada 1800–1914* (Toronto: University of Toronto Press, 1997), 24–43.

60 Axelrod, *The Promise of Schooling*, 25.

61 Axelrod, 25.

62 Solomon and Portelli, "Introduction," 18; Laura Pinto, *Curriculum Reform in Ontario: "Common Sense" Policy Processes and Democratic Possibilities* (Toronto: University of Toronto Press, 2012), 35.

63 Pinto, *Curriculum Reform in Ontario*, 6.

64 Nancy Fraser, "Reframing Justice in a Globalizing World," *New Left Review* II, no. 36 (2005): 73–4.

65 Richard Wilkinson and Kate Pickett, *The Spirit Level: Why Greater Equality Makes Societies Stronger* (New York: Bloomsbury USA, 2011): 84.

66 Wilkinson and Pickett, *The Spirit Level*, 52–6.

2. Researching Education Privatization: Traditional and Critical Approaches

1 Carol Campbell et al., *Ontario: A Learning Province: Findings and Recommendations from the Independent Review of Assessment and Reporting* (Toronto: Government of Ontario, March 2018).

2 Laura-Lee Kearns, "High-Stakes Standardized Testing and Marginalized Youth: An Examination of the Impact on Those Who Fail," *Canadian Journal of Education* 34, no. 2 (2011): 112–30.

3 Kearns, "High-Stakes Standardized Testing," 118.

4 Kearns, 126.

5 Hanna Wickstrom, Ellen Fesseha, and Eunice Eunhee Jang, "Examining the Relation Between IEP Status, Testing Accommodations, and Elementary Students' EQAO Mathematics Achievement," *Canadian Journal of Science, Mathematics and Technology Education* 20, no. 2 (1 June 2020): 297–311, https://doi.org/10.1007/s42330-020-00088-5.

6 Wickstrom, Fesseha, and Jang, "Examining the Relation," 308.

7 Kearns, "High-Stakes Standardized Testing," 127.

8 Stephen J. Ball and Deborah Youdell, *Hidden Privatisation in Public Education: Preliminary Report* (Brussels: Education International Brussels, 2007), https://pages.ei-ie.org/quadrennialreport/2007/upload/content_trsl_images/630/Hidden_privatisation-EN.pdf.

9 Maarten Simons, Mark Olssen, and Michael Peters, "Part 1: The Critical Education Policy Orientation," in *Re-Reading Education Policies: A Handbook Studying the Policy Agenda of the 21st Century*, ed. Maarten Simons, Mark Olssen, and Michael Peters (Boston: Sense Publishers, 2009), 1–35.

10 Simons, Olssen, and Peters, "Part 1," 1.

11 Michelle D. Young and Sarah Diem, "Doing Critical Policy Analysis in Education Research: An Emerging Paradigm," in *Complementary Research Methods for Educational Leadership and Policy Studies*, ed. Chad R. Lochmiller (Cham: Springer International Publishing, 2018), 79–98, https://doi.org/10.1007/978-3-319-93539-3_5; John A. Codd, "The Construction and Deconstruction of Educational Policy Documents," *Journal of Education Policy* 3, no. 3 (1 July 1988), 237; Megan M. Chase et al., "Transfer Equity for 'Minoritized' Students: A Critical Policy Analysis of Seven States," *Educational Policy* 28, no. 5 (1 September 2014): 673, https://doi.org/10.1177/0895904812468227.

12 Deborah Stone, *Policy Paradox: The Art of Political Decision Making*, Revised (New York: W.W. Norton, 2002), 8.

13 Werner Jann and Kai Wegrich, "Theories of the Policy Cycle," in *Handbook of Public Policy Analysis: Theory, Politics, and Methods*, ed. Frank Fischer, Gerald J. Miller, and Mara S. Sidney (Boca Raton, FL: CRC Press, 2007): 45–55.

14 Meredith I. Honig, "Complexity and Policy Implementation: Challenges and Opportunities for the Field," in *New Directions in Policy Implementation: Confronting Complexity*, ed. Meredith I. Honig, (Albany, NY: State University of New York, 2006), 2.

15 Lorraine M. McDonnell and Richard F. Elmore, "Getting the Job Done: Alternative Policy Instruments," *Educational Evaluation and Policy Analysis* 9, no. 2 (1 June 1987): 133, https://doi.org/10.3102/01623737009002133.

16 Jann and Wengrich, "Theories," 56.

17 Murray Edelman, *Constructing the Political Spectacle* (Chicago: University of Chicago Press, 1988), 8; Frank Fischer and Herbert Gottweis, "Introduction: The Argumentative Turn Revisited," in *The Argumentative Turn Revisited: Public Policy as Communicative Practice*, ed. Frank Fischer and Herbert Gottweis (Durham, NC: Duke University Press, 2012), 6.

18 Stephen. J. Ball, *Politics and Policy Making in Education: Explorations in Policy Sociology* (London: Routledge, 1990), 6.

19 Sonya Douglass Horsford, Janelle T. Scott, and Gary L. Anderson, *The Politics of Education Policy in an Era of Inequality* (New York: Routledge, 2019), 40–1.

20 Sarah Diem et al., "The Intellectual Landscape of Critical Policy Analysis," *International Journal of Qualitative Studies in Education* 27, no. 9 (21 October 2014): 1068–90, https://doi.org/10.1080/09518398.2014.916007, 1072.

21 Stephanie Schroeder, Elizabeth Currin, and Todd McCardle, "Mother Tongues: The Opt Out Movement's Vocal Response to Patriarchal, Neoliberal Education Reform," *Gender and Education* 30, no. 8 (17 November 2018): 1010, https://doi.org/10.1080/09540253.2016.1270422.

22 Laura Elizabeth Pinto, "Tensions and Fissures: The Politics of Standardised Testing and Accountability in Ontario, 1995–2015," *The Curriculum Journal* 27, no. 1 (2 January 2016): 97, https://doi.org/10.1080/09585176.2016.1140061.

23 Pinto, "Tensions and Fissures," 98.

24 Goli M. Rezai-Rashti and Allison Segeren, "The Game of Accountability: Perspectives of Urban School Leaders on Standardized Testing in Ontario and British Columbia, Canada," *International Journal of Leadership in Education*, published under latest articles 15 November 2020, https://doi.org/10.1080/13603124.2020.1808711.

25 Bradley A.U. Levinson, Margaret Sutton, and Teresa Winstead, "Education Policy as a Practice of Power: Theoretical Tools, Ethnographic Methods, Democratic Options," *Educational Policy* 23, no. 6 (2009): 767–95.
26 Annette Braun et al., "Taking Context Seriously: Towards Explaining Policy Enactments in the Secondary School," *Discourse: Studies in the Cultural Politics of Education* 32, no. 4 (2011): 586.
27 Levinson, Sutton, and Winstead, "Taking Context Seriously," 768.
28 Levinson, Sutton, and Winstead, 768.
29 Cameron Graham and Dean Neu, "Standardized Testing and the Construction of Governable Persons," *Journal of Curriculum Studies* 36, no. 3 (1 May 2004): 295–319, https://doi.org/10.1080/0022027032000167080.
30 Graham and Neu, "Standardized Testing," 298.
31 Richard Bowe, Stephen J. Ball, and Anne Gold, *Reforming Education and Changing Schools: Case Studies in Policy Sociology* (New York: Routledge, 1992), 19–23.

3. Funding Advantage in Public Schools

1 People for Education, *2019 Annual Report on Schools: What Makes a School?* (Toronto: People for Education, 2019), https://peopleforeducation.ca/report/2019-annual-report-on-schools-what-makes-a-school/.
2 Bernie Froese-Germain et al., *Commercialism in Canadian Schools: Who's Calling the Shots?* (Ottawa: Canadian Centre for Policy Alternatives, 2006), 12.
3 Toronto District School Board, "2016 Snapshot of School Council Operations in the Toronto District School Board," 16/17-10 (Toronto: Toronto District School Board, January 2017): 14.
4 Shane Magee, "Province's New Nutrition Policy Leaves School Fundraisers in Lurch," CBC, 31 August 2018, https://www.cbc.ca/news/canada/new-brunswick/policy-711-eliminates-low-nutrition-food-1.4806257.
5 CBC News, "7 Things to Know about School Fundraising in Calgary," CBC, 7 September 2013, https://www.cbc.ca/news/canada/calgary/7-things-to-know-about-school-fundraising-in-calgary-1.1703579.
6 CBC News, "Edmonton Catholic Schools Lose Casino Fundraising," CBC, 3 December 2009, https://www.cbc.ca/news/canada/edmonton/edmonton-catholic-schools-lose-casino-fundraising-1.843292.
7 People for Education, *2019 Annual Report.*
8 Lord Tennyson Elementary PAC, "Kick-Start Campaign," 2019, http://www.lordtennyson.ca/kick-start-campaign.html.

9 The Canadian Press, "Fundraising Site for Nunavut Greenhouse Draws Dollars, Encouragement and Advice," CityNews Toronto, 23 May 2017, https://toronto.citynews.ca/2017/05/23/fundraising-site-for-nunavut -greenhouse-draws-dollars-encouragement-and-advice/.

10 Amy Judd, "Elementary School Teacher Sets up Crowdfunding Page for Classroom Supplies," Global News, 22 September 2014, https:// globalnews.ca/news/1577029/elementary-school-teacher-sets-up -crowdfunding-page-for-classroom-supplies/.

11 CTV News, "More than Half Sask. Teachers Spend $500 of Own Money on Classroom Costs: STF," CTV, 30 August 2019, https://saskatoon .ctvnews.ca/more-than-half-sask-teachers-spend-500-of-own-money-on -classroom-costs-stf-1.4572851.

12 CBC News, "Tax Breaks Urged for Teachers Buying School Supplies," CBC, 26 August 2013, https://www.cbc.ca/news/canada/nova-scotia /tax-breaks-urged-for-teachers-buying-school-supplies-1.1303581.

13 Nova Scotia Department of Education and Nova Scotia Department of Health Promotion and Protection, "Food and Nutrition Policy for Nova Scotia Public Schools" (Halifax: Government of Nova Scotia, 2006), 5.

14 Newfoundland and Labrador, *Schools Act, 1997*, SNL 1997 c S-12.2, https://www.assembly.nl.ca/legislation/sr/statutes/s12-2.htm.

15 Department of Education and Early Childhood Development, "Policy 132: Contribution of Resources by Parents" (Fredericton: Government of New Brunswick, 1 September 1999), 1, https://www2.gnb.ca/content /gnb/en/departments/education/k12/content/policies.html.

16 Department of Education and Early Childhood Development, "Policy 132," 2.

17 Ontario Ministry of Education, *Fundraising Guideline* (Toronto: Queen's Printer for Ontario, 2012), 3–5, http://www.edu.gov.on.ca/eng/parents /fundraising.html.

18 Ontario Ministry of Education, *Fundraising Guideline*, 4.

19 People for Education, *2019 Annual Report*.

20 Yukon Education, "Fund Raising in Schools Policy" (Whitehorse: Yukon Education, 1 April 2015), 2.

21 People for Education, *2019 Annual Report*.

22 Patty Winsa, "Toronto Schools Raise Less Money than Rest of Region," *Toronto Star*, 3 September 2016, https://www.thestar.com/yourtoronto /education/2016/09/03/toronto-schools-raise-less-money-than-rest-of -region.html.

23 Toronto District School Board, "Toronto District School Board 2014–15 and 2015–2016 School Budget and School Generated Funds," Finance,

Budget and Enrolment Committee (Toronto: Toronto District School Board, 10 May 2017), 2–14.

24 Patty Winsa, "As Fundraising Gap Grows, Toronto's Wealthy Schools Leaving Poor Schools behind," *Toronto Star*, 11 April 2015, http://www .thestar.com/yourtoronto/education/2015/04/11/as-fundraising-gap -grows-torontos-wealthy-schools-leaving-poor-schools-behind.html.

25 Vana Pistiolis, *The Results and Implications of Fundraising in Elementary Public Schools: Interviews with Ontario Principals* (Toronto: Ontario Institute for Studies in Education of the University of Toronto, 2012).

26 People for Education, *2019 Annual Report.*

27 Arik Ligeti, "Fundraising Playing Key Role at Some of Vancouver's Poorest Schools," *Globe and Mail*, 20 February 2015, https://www .theglobeandmail.com/news/british-columbia/donations-subsidizing -programs-playgrounds-at-some-of-vancouvers-poorest-schools /article23138649/.

28 Toronto District School Board, "Policy P021: Fundraising" (Toronto: Toronto District School Board, 26 June 2003), 1.

29 Sharma Queiser, *Missing Opportunities: How Budget Policies Continue to Leave behind Low-Income Students* (Toronto: Social Planning Toronto, 2017), 1.

30 Kristin Rushowy, "Schools Forced to Use More Volunteers," *Toronto Star*, 2000, A9.

31 Hugh Mackenzie, *Harris-Era Hangovers: Toronto School Trustees' Inherited Funding Shortfall* (Ottawa: Canadian Centre for Policy Alternatives, 2015), 5, www.policyalternatives.ca/publications/reports/harris-era-hangovers; Hugh Mackenzie, *Shortchanging Ontario Students: An Overview and Assessment of Education Funding in Ontario* (Toronto: Elementary Teachers' Federation of Ontario, 2017), 2.

32 Toronto District School Board, *2017–2018 Fundraising Guide* (Toronto: Toronto District School Board, 2017), 1.

33 Linn Posey-Maddox, "Professionalizing the PTO: Race, Class and Shifting Norms of Parental Engagement in a City Public School," *American Journal of Education* 119, no. 2 (2013): 253, https://doi.org/10.1086/668754.

34 Posey-Maddox, "Professionalizing the PTO," 251.

35 Linn Posey-Maddox, "Beyond the Consumer: Parents, Privatization, and Fundraising in US Urban Public Schooling," *Journal of Education Policy* 31, no. 2 (3 March 2016): 178–97, https://doi.org/10.1080/02680939.2015.1065345.

36 Alexandra Freidus, "'Great School Benefits Us All': Advantaged Parents and the Gentrification of an Urban Public School," *Urban Education* 54, no. 8 (2019): 1133, https://doi.org/10.1177/0042085916636656.

37 Bronwyn Davies and Peter Bansel, "Neoliberalism and Education," *International Journal of Qualitative Studies in Education* 20, no. 3 (May 2007): 251.

38 Carol Vincent and Stephen J. Ball, "'Making up' the Middle-Class Child: Families, Activities and Class Dispositions," *Sociology* 41, no. 6 (12 January 2007): 1062, https://doi.org/10.1177/0038038507082315.

39 Joseph Di Bona et al., "Commercialism in North Carolina High Schools: A Survey of Principals' Perceptions," *Peabody Journal of Education* 78, no. 2 (1 April 2003): 56, https://doi.org/10.1207/S15327930PJE7802_03.

40 Brian O. Brent and Stephen Lunden, "Much Ado about Very Little: The Benefits and Costs of School-Based Commercial Activities," *Leadership and Policy in Schools* 8, no. 3 (2009): 319.

41 Government of New Brunswick, *Education Act*, SNB 1997, c E-1.12, http://laws.gnb.ca/en/ShowTdm/cs/E-1.12.

42 Department of Education and Early Childhood Development, "Policy 132," 2.

43 Manitoba Education, "Finance and Statistics," Manitoba Education, November 1998, https://www.edu.gov.mb.ca/k12/finance/feepolicy.html.

44 Lord Byng Secondary School, "2019/20 School Fees," Families, 27 August 2019, 1, https://www.vsb.bc.ca:443/schools/lord-byng/Families/Fees/Pages/Default.aspx.

45 People for Education, *2019 Annual Report*.

46 C.S. Mott Children's Hospital, "Pay-to-Participate Limiting School Activities for Lower-Income Students," National Poll on Children's Health, 17 October 2016, https://mottpoll.org/reports-surveys/pay-participate-limiting-school-activities-lower-income-students.

47 Community Services Council Newfoundland and Labrador, "Expanding Their Universe, Reshaping Their Future: A Report on the Impact of School Fees and Fundraising on Social Inclusion," 2003, 2–18, http://communitysector.nl.ca/publications/all.

48 Lord Byng Secondary School, "2019/20 School Fees," 2–3.

49 Lord Byng Secondary School, 1.

50 Delta Golf Academy, "Application Process," Apply, n.d., https://deltagolfacademy.com/home/apply/.

51 TDSB Enhancing Equity Task Force, *TDSB Enhancing Equity Task Force Report* (Draft) (Toronto: TDSB, 24 October 2017), 29.

52 Lord Byng Secondary School, "2019/20 School Fees," 1.

53 Manitoba Education, "Finance and Statistics."

54 Department of Education and Early Childhood Development, "Policy 132: Contribution of Resources by Parents" (Fredericton: Government of New Brunswick, 1 September 1999), 4, https://www2.gnb.ca/content /gnb/en/departments/education/k12/content/policies.html.
55 British Columbia Teachers Federation, "Poverty and Education Survey: A Teacher's Perspective," 2012, 17, https://www.bctf.ca/PovertyResearch .aspx.
56 C.S. Mott Children's Hospital, "Pay-to-Participate: Impact on School Activities," National Poll on Children's Health, 18 March 2019, https:// mottpoll.org/reports/pay-participate-impact-school-activities.
57 Calgary Board of Education, "Fees & Waivers," 2020, https://cbe.ab .ca/registration/fees-and-waivers/Pages/default.aspx.
58 Calgary Board of Education, "Waivers," 2020, https://cbe.ab.ca /registration/fees-and-waivers/Pages/Waivers.aspx.
59 Sue Winton and Michelle Milani, "Policy Advocacy, Inequity, and School Fees and Fundraising in Ontario, Canada," *Education Policy Analysis Archives* 25, no. 40 (24 April 2017): 5, https://doi.org/10.14507/epaa.25.2679.
60 Rajani Naidoo, "Competition in Higher Education," FreshEd with Will Brehm, accessed 6 August 2020, https://freshedpodcast.com /rajaninaidoo/.
61 Equity and Inclusivity Advisory Committee Classism/Poverty Sub-Committee, *Conversation Feedback and Recommendations* (Aurora, ON: York Region District School Board, April 2018), 16.
62 CBC News, "Quebec Mother's Class-Action Lawsuit against School Fees to Go Ahead," CBC, 8 December 2016, https://www.cbc.ca/news /canada/montreal/quebec-school-board-fees-lawsuit-1.3886869.
63 "Notice of Court Approval of a Transaction," Cision, 8 December 2018, https://www.newswire.ca/news-releases/notice-of-court-approval-of -a-transaction-702238261.html.
64 Ministère de l'Éducation et de l'Enseignement supérieur, "Summary: Results of the Public Consultation on School Fees" (Quebec: Gouvernement du Québec, 21 February 2019): 3, http://www.education.gouv.qc.ca/en /references/tx-solrtyperecherchepublicationtx-solrpublicationnouveaute /results/detail/article/summary-results-of-the-public-consultation -on-school-fees-1/.
65 Ministère de l'Éducation et de l'Enseignement supérieur, "Memory Aid," School Fees – Memory Aid, 20 June 2019, 1, http://www.education.gouv. qc.ca/en/references/tx-solrtyperecherchepublicationtx-solrpublication nouveaute/results/detail/article/school-fees-memory-aid/?a =a&cHash=46cb695d5c5c6cbf0e3164ec9c3b7216.

66 Wendy Poole and Gerald Fallon, "The Emerging Fourth Tier in K–12 Education Finance in British Columbia, Canada: Increasing Privatisation and Implications for Social Justice," *Globalisation, Societies and Education* 13, no. 3 (2015): 347.

67 Canadian Bureau for International Education, "International Students in Canada," 2020, https://cbie.ca/infographic/.

68 Government of British Columbia, *British Columbia's International Education Strategy* (Victoria: Government of British Columbia, 2012), 1; Roslyn Kunin & Associates, Inc., *An Assessment of the Economic Impact of International Education in British Columbia: An Update in 2017* (Vancouver: British Columbia Council for International Education, May 2019), 13, https://bccie.bc.ca/resources/reports-publications/.

69 Toronto District School Board, *Financial Facts: Revenue and Expenditure Trends* (Toronto: Toronto District School Board, 2019), 6.

70 Canadian Bureau for International Education, "International Students in Canada."

71 Toronto Catholic District School Board, *International Education Update Report: Corporate Services, Strategic Planning and Property Committee* (Toronto: Toronto Catholic District School Board, 14 April 2016), 221–3, https://www.tcdsb.org/Board/TrusteesoftheBoard/Committees/Pages/Corporate-Services-April-14-2016.aspx.

72 Alberta Government, *Alberta's International Strategy 2013* (Edmonton: Government of Alberta, 2013), 31.

73 British Columbia Ministry of Education, "International Education Information for Administrators – Province of British Columbia," Government of British Columbia, n.d., https://www2.gov.bc.ca/gov/content/education-training/k-12/administration/program-management/international-education.

74 Government of Ontario, Ministry of Education, *Ontario's Strategy for K–12 International Education* (Toronto: Government of Ontario, 2015), 2.

75 Alberta Government, "Economic and Social Impact," 2.

76 Roslyn Kunin & Associates, Inc., 13, https://bccie.bc.ca/resources/reports-publications/.

77 Johanna L. Waters, "Emergent Geographies of International Education and Social Exclusion," *Antipode* 38, no. 5 (2006): 1062, https://doi.org/10.1111/j.1467-8330.2006.00492.x.

78 Wendy Poole, Gerald Fallon, and Vicheth Sen, "Privatised Sources of Funding and the Spatiality of Inequities in Public Education," *Journal of Educational Administration and History* 52, no. 1 (2 January 2020): 130, https://doi.org/10.1080/00220620.2019.1689105.

79 Alberta Government, "Economic and Social Impact of International
     K-12 Students on Alberta" (Alberta Government, May 2017), 4, https://
     www.alberta.ca/international-education-programs.aspx#toc-1.
80 Ryan Deschambault, "Fee-Paying English Language Learners: Situating
     International Students' Impact on British Columbia's Public Schools,"
     *Canadian Journal of Applied Linguistics / Revue Canadienne de Linguistique
     Appliquée* 21, no. 2 (2018): 61.
81 Merli Tamtik and Angela O'Brien-Klewchuk, "The Political Process of
     International Education: Complementarities and Clashes in the Manitoba
     K–12 Sector through a Multi-Level Governance Lens," *Education Policy
     Analysis Archives* 28, no. 1 (6 January 2020): 9, https://doi.org/10.14507
     /epaa.28.4609.
82 Tamtik and O'Brien-Klewchuk, "The Political Process," 12–13.
83 Waters, "Emergent Geographies," 1051–3.

4. Securing Private Benefits

1 Christopher Lubienski, "School Choice and Privatization in Education:
     An Alternative Analytical Framework," *Journal for Critical Education Pol-
     icy Studies* 4, no. 1 (2006): 273, http://www.jceps.com/archives/511.
 2 Janelle T. Scott, "Market-Driven Education Reform and the Racial Pol-
     itics of Advocacy," *Peabody Journal of Education* 86, no. 5 (1 November
     2011): 585, https://doi.org/10.1080/0161956X.2011.616445.
 3 Scott Davies and Janice Aurini, "Exploring School Choice in Canada:
     Who Chooses What and Why?" *Canadian Public Policy / Analyse de poli-
     tiques* 37, no. 4 (2011): 467.
 4 Ee-Seul Yoon and Christopher Lubienski, "How Do Marginalized Fami-
     lies Engage in School Choice in Inequitable Urban Landscapes? A Criti-
     cal Geographic Approach," *Education Policy Analysis Archives* 25, no. 42
     (24 April 2017): 10–11, http://eric.ed.gov/?id=EJ1141831.
 5 See also Ee-Seul Yoon and Lyn D. Daniels, "At the Margins of Canada:
     School Choice Practices of Aboriginal Families in a Settler-Colonial
     City," *Educational Policy* 35, no. 7 (2021): 1288–1310, https://doi.org
     /10.1177/0895904819864442.
 6 Andreu Termes, D. Brent Edwards, and Antoni Verger, "The Develop-
     ment and Dynamics of Public-Private Partnerships in the Philippines'
     Education: A Counterintuitive Case of School Choice, Competition, and
     Privatization," *Educational Policy* 34, no. 1 (1 January 2020): 113, https://
     doi.org/10.1177/0895904819886323; Sietske Waslander, Cissy Pater, and
     Maartje van der Weide, "Markets in Education: An Analytical Review of

Empirical Research on Market Mechanisms in Education" (OECD Education Working Papers No. 52, OECD iLibrary, Paris, France, 21 October 2010), 66, https://doi.org/10.1787/5km4pskmkr27-en.

7 Emma E. Rowe and Christopher Lubienski, "Shopping for Schools or Shopping for Peers: Public Schools and Catchment Area Segregation," *Journal of Education Policy* 32, no. 3 (4 May 2017): 352, https://doi.org/10.1080/02680939.2016.1263363.

8 Kate Hammer, "Toronto Parents up in Arms over Proposed School Boundary Change," *Globe ana Mail*, 21 September 2014, https://www.theglobeandmail.com/news/toronto/toronto-parents-up-in-arms-over-proposed-school-boundary-change/article20714740/.

9 Saahoon Hong and Wonseok Choi, "A Longitudinal Analysis of the Effects of Open Enrollment on Equity and Academic Achievement: Evidence from Minneapolis, Minnesota," *Children and Youth Services Review* 49 (1 February 2015): 66, https://doi.org/10.1016/j.childyouth.2015.01.002; Kristie J.R. Phillips, Charles Hausman, and Elisabeth S. Larsen. "Students Who Choose and the Schools They Leave: Examining Participation in Intradistrict Transfers," *The Sociological Quarterly* 53, no. 2 (2012): 282–3, https://doi.org/10.1111/j.1533-8525.2012.01234.x.

10 Valerie Ledwith, "The Influence of Open Enrollment on Scholastic Achievement among Public School Students in Los Angeles," *American Journal of Education* 116, no. 2 (1 February 2010): 252, https://doi.org/10.1086/649493.

11 Lesley Lavery and Deven Carlson, "Dynamic Participation in Interdistrict Open Enrollment," *Educational Policy* 29, no. 5 (July 2015): 771–2, https://doi.org/10.1177/0895904813518103.

12 Phillips, Hausman, and Larsen, "Students Who Choose," 284.

13 Kristie J.R. Phillips, Elisabeth S. Larsen, and Charles Hausman, "School Choice and Social Stratification: How Intra-District Transfers Shift the Racial/Ethnic and Economic Composition of Schools," *Social Science Research* 51 (1 May 2015): 47, https://doi.org/10.1016/j.ssresearch.2014.12.005.

14 Amy Stuart Wells, Lauren Fox, and Diana Cordova-Cobo, "How Racially Diverse Schools and Classrooms Can Benefit All Students" (New York: The Century Foundation, 9 February 2016): 12, https://tcf.org/content/report/how-racially-diverse-schools-and-classrooms-can-benefit-all-students/.

15 Jason Ellis and Ee-Seul Yoon, "From Alternative Schools to School Choice in the Vancouver School District, 1960s to the Neoliberal Present," *Canadian Journal of Educational Administration and Policy* 88 (7 April 2019): 87, https://m.jmss.org/index.php/cjeap/article/view/43357.

16 Toronto District School Board, "Africentric Alternative School," n.d., https://schoolweb.tdsb.on.ca/africentricschool.

17 Kalervo N. Gulson and P. Taylor Webb, "Not Just Another Alternative School: Policy Problematization, Neoliberalism, and Racial Biopolitics," *Educational Policy* 30, no. 1 (1 January 2016): 155–6, https://doi.org/10.1177/0895904815615438.

18 Philip S.S. Howard and Carl E. James, "When Dreams Take Flight: How Teachers Imagine and Implement an Environment That Nurtures Blackness at an Africentric School in Toronto, Ontario," *Curriculum Inquiry* 49, no. 3 (2019): 322, https://doi.org/10.1080/03626784.2019.1614879.

19 Carl E. James et al., *Africentric Alternative School Research Project; Year 3 (2013–14)* (Toronto: York University's Centre for Education and Community and the Toronto District School Board, 2014), 16.

20 Ellis and Yoon, "From Alternative Schools," 86.

21 Julia Resnik, "All against All Competition: The Incorporation of the International Baccalaureate in Public High Schools in Canada," *Journal of Education Policy* 35, no. 3 (3 May 2020): 317, https://doi.org/10.1080/02680939.2018.1562105.

22 Jia Wang, Joan L. Herman, and Daniel Dockterman, "A Research Synthesis of Magnet School Effect on Student Outcomes: Beyond Descriptive Studies," *Journal of School Choice* 12, no. 2 (3 April 2018): 173, https://doi.org/10.1080/15582159.2018.1440100.

23 Julie C. Harris, "Changing Context: Do Magnet Schools Improve Student Achievement in a Modern Setting?" *Journal of School Choice* 13, no. 3 (3 July 2019): 305–34, https://doi.org/10.1080/15582159.2019.1594605.

24 Vancouver School Board, "Mini School Application Process," Secondary Programs, 2020, https://www.vsb.bc.ca:443/Student_Learning/Secondary/Mini_Schools/Pages/Default.aspx.

25 Rubén Gaztambide-Fernández and Gillian Parekh, "Market 'Choices' or Structured Pathways? How Specialized Arts Education Contributes to the Reproduction of Inequality," *Education Policy Analysis Archives* 25, no. 41 (24 April 2017): 6, https://doi.org/10.14507/epaa.25.2716.

26 Gillian Parekh, Isabel Killoran, and Cameron Crawford, "The Toronto Connection: Poverty, Perceived Ability, and Access to Education Equity," *Canadian Journal of Education* 34, no. 3 (2011): 274.

27 Conseil supérieur de l'éducation, *Steering the Course Back to Equity in Education; Report of the State and Needs of Education 2014–2016* (Quebec: Government of Quebec, September 2016), 1.

28 Yoon and Daniels, "At the Margins," 18.

29 FACE School, "Registration: Admissions Criteria," FACE School, 2020, 1.

30 FACE School, 2.

31 Gaztambide-Fernández and Gillian Parekh, "Market 'Choices' or Structured Pathways," 4.

32 Lynn Bosetti and Dianne Gereluk, *Understanding School Choice in Canada* (Toronto: University of Toronto Press, 2016), 45.

33 Ministry of Education, "French Immersion Program," Government of British Columbia, n.d., https://www2.gov.bc.ca/gov/content/education -training/k-12/administration/legislation-policy/public-schools /french-immersion-program.

34 Manitoba Education, "French Immersion Program," n.d., https://www .edu.gov.mb.ca/k12/cur/fr_imm_pr.html.

35 Canadian Parents for French, "French as a Second Language Enrolment Statistics: 2015–2016 to 2019–2020" (Ottawa: Canadian Parents for French, n.d.): 3, https://cpf.ca/wp-content/uploads/CPF_Nat _EnrolmentStats-2019-2020.pdf.

36 Tracy Sherlock, "Annual Lineups Begin for B.C. French Immersion Spots," *Vancouver Sun*, 6 February 2014, https://vancouversun.com /news/metro/annual-lineups-begin-for-bc-french-immersion-spots.

37 Riley Laychuk, "French Immersion Lottery Frustrates French-Speaking Manitoba Family," CBC, 30 December 2016, https://www .cbc.ca/news/canada/manitoba/brandon-french-Immersion -complaint-1.3915751.

38 E. Sinay, *Research Brief on the Characteristics of Students in the French as a Second Language Programs at the Toronto District School Board* (Toronto: Toronto District School Board, 2015), 4–6.

39 Gillian Parekh, "Selected In-School Programs," 3–5.

40 Ottawa-Carleton District School Board, *Status of English with Core French Program* (Ottawa: Ottawa-Carleton District School Board, 2019).

41 Ottawa-Carleton District School Board, *Status*, 8.

42 Parekh, Killoran, and Crawford, "The Toronto Connection," 258.

43 Ee-Seul Yoon and Kalervo N. Gulson, "School Choice in the Stratilingual City of Vancouver," *British Journal of Sociology of Education* 31, no. 6 (2010): 715.

44 Renée Christine Bourgoin, "French Immersion: 'So Why Would You Do Something Like That to a Child?': Issues of Advocacy, Accessibility, and Inclusion," *International Journal of Bias, Identity and Diversities in Education (IJBIDE)* 1, no. 1 (1 January 2016): 50, https://doi.org/10.4018 /IJBIDE.2016010104.

45 Beyhan Farhadi, "'The Sky's the Limit': On the Impossible Promise of E-Learning in the Toronto District School Board" (PhD diss., University of Toronto, 2019), https://hdl.handle.net/1807/97442.

46 Ministry of Education, "Online Learning," Government of British Colum-
    bia, 2021, https://www2.gov.bc.ca/gov/content/education
    -training/k-12/support/classroom-alternatives/online-learning.

47 Larry Kuehn, *BC Education Privatization through Distributed Learning*,
    BCTF Research Report (Vancouver: BCTF, 2018) (No. 2018-RR-02), 5,
    https://www.bctf.ca/docs/default-source/default-document-library
    /rr2018-02-(1).pdf?sfvrsn=11cb0376_0.

48 Larry Kuehn, *The Many Faces of Privatization*, BCTF Research Report
    (Vancouver: BCTF, 2019), 11, https://www.bctf.ca/docs/default-source
    /for-news-and-stories/report94b639b6e4d1484a904ee82f97462d04
    .pdf?sfvrsn=986771f8_0.

49 CBC News, "Ontario High School Students Must Take 2 Mandatory Online
    Courses before Graduation," CBC, 21 November 2019, https://www.cbc
    .ca/news/canada/toronto/high-school-students-mandatory-online
    -courses-graduation-1.5368305.

50 Joseph R. Friedhoff, *Michigan's K–12 Virtual Learning Effectiveness Report,
    2017–18*, Michigan Virtual, 27 March 2019, https://michiganvirtual.org
    /research/publications/michigans-k-12-virtual-learning-effectiveness
    -report-2017-18/.

51 Nikki Herta, "How Effective Is Online Learning in Michigan," Michigan
    Virtual, 23 April 2018, https://michiganvirtual.org/blog/how-effective
    -is-online-learning-in-michigan/.

52 Karissa Donkin, "More than 1,300 N.B. Students Not Reached by Schools
    during Pandemic," CBC, 16 June 2020, https://www.cbc.ca/news
    /canada/new-brunswick/covid-students-reached-schools-1.5612341.

53 Beth Macdonell, "How 20,000 Students Are Being Connected to Educa-
    tion during the Pandemic," CTV News Toronto, 20 April 2020, https://
    toronto.ctvnews.ca/how-20-000-students-are-being-connected-to
    -education-during-the-pandemic-1.4904607.

54 Lynn Bosetti and Michael C. Pyryt, "Parental Motivation in School
    Choice," *Journal of School Choice* 1, no. 4 (1 March 2007): 105, https://
    doi.org/10.1300/15582150802098795.

55 "New Horizons Charter School Society Charter Document (Final),"
    2012, 2, https://www.newhorizons.ca/wp-content/uploads/2016/08
    /NHCSS-CHARTER-2012-FINAL-with-required-changes-accepted.pdf.

56 Alison Taylor, *The Politics of Educational Reform in Alberta* (Toronto: Uni-
    versity of Toronto Press, 2001): 3, https://books.scholarsportal.info
    /uri/ebooks/ebooks0/gibson_crkn/2009-12-01/6/418124.

57 Lynn Bosetti and Phil Butterfield, "The Politics of Educational Reform:
    The Alberta Charter School Experiment 20 Years Later," *Global Education
    Review* 3, no. 2 (2016): 103.

58 Alberta Education, *Charter Schools Handbook* (Edmonton, AB: Alberta Government, 2015), 4, https://open.alberta.ca/publications /edc-charter-schools-handbook.

59 Government of Alberta, "Student Population Statistics," 2020, https:// www.alberta.ca/student-population-statistics.aspx.

60 Bosetti and Butterfield, "The Politics of Educational Reform," 103–4.

61 Doug Archbald, Andrew Hurwitz, and Felicia Hurwitz, "Charter Schools, Parent Choice, and Segregation: A Longitudinal Study of the Growth of Charters and Changing Enrollment Patterns in Five School Districts over 26 Years," *Education Policy Analysis Archives* 26, no. 22 (19 February 2018): 29–31, https://doi.org/10.14507/epaa.26.2921.

62 Peggy Sattler, "Education Governance Reform in Ontario: Neoliberalism in Context," *Canadian Journal of Educational Administration and Policy* 128 (2012): 5.

63 L.W. Downey, "The Aid-to-Independent-Schools Movement in British Columbia," in *Schools in the West: Essays in Canadian Educational History*, ed. Nancy M. Sheehan, J. Donald Wilson, and David C. Jones (Calgary: Detselig Enterprises, 1986), 305–9; J.J. Stapleton and J.C. Long, "The Manitoba Independent Schools Question, 1957–1996," in *St. Paul's College: Memories and Histories*, ed. Gerald Friesen and Richard Lebrun (Winnipeg: St. Paul's College, 1999), 304–24.

64 Kuehn, *The Many Faces of Privatization*, 8–9.

65 J.J. Bergen, "The Private School Movement in Alberta," *Alberta Journal of Educational Research* 28, no. 4 (1982): 320; M. Wagner, "Charter Schools in Alberta: Change or Continuity in Progressive Conservative Education Policy? *Alberta Journal of Educational Research* 45, no. 1 (1999): 57; Sue Winton, and Steven Staples, "Shifting Meanings: The Struggle over Public Funding of Private Schools in Alberta, Canada," *Education Policy Analysis Archives* 30 (8 February 2022): 5, https://doi .org/10.14507/epaa.30.7002.

66 Jean Barman, "Deprivatizing Private Education: The British Columbia Experience," *Canadian Journal of Education / Revue canadienne de l'éducation* 16, no. 1 (1991): 12, https://doi.org/10.2307/1495214.

67 Jean Barman, "Deprivatizing Private Education," 16.

68 Canada Revenue Agency, "Tuition Fees and Charitable Donations Paid to Privately Supported Secular and Religious Schools," 22 June 2017, https://www.canada.ca/en/revenue-agency/services/forms-publications /publications/ic75-23/tuition-fees-charitable-donations-paid -privately-supported-secular-religious-schools.html.

69 Bosetti and Pyryt, "Parental Motivation," 97.

70 Jerry Paquette, "Public Funding for 'Private' Education: The Equity Challenge of Enhanced Choice," *American Journal of Education* 111, no. 4 (2005): 568, https://doi.org/10.1086/431184.

71 Termes, Edwards, and Verger, "The Development and Dynamics," 92.

72 "Children First: School Choice Trust," 2012, http://www .childrenfirstgrants.ca/.

73 V. Gentles, *The School Choice Experience: Findings of the Children First: School Choice Trust Parent Survey*, Studies in Education Policy (Vancouver: The Fraser Institute, 2004), 2.

74 Waslander, Pater, and van der Weide, "Markets in Education," 13.

75 R. Joseph Waddington and Mark Berends, "Impact of the Indiana Choice Scholarship Program: Achievement Effects for Students in Upper Elementary and Middle School," *Journal of Policy Analysis and Management* 37, no. 4 (Fall 2018): 797, https://doi.org/10.1002/pam.22086.

76 Waslander, Pater, and van der Weide, "Markets in Education," 11.

77 United Conservative Party, "United Conservative Party: Member Policy Declaration as Approved on Dec. 1, 2019," 1 December 2020, 10, https://unitedconservative.ca/About.

78 Janice Aurini and Scott Davies, "Choice without Markets: Homeschooling in the Context of Private Education," *British Journal of Sociology of Education* 26, no. 4 (1 January 2005): 466–7, https://doi.org/10.1080 /01425690500199834.

79 Statistics Canada, "Number and Proportion of Students in Elementary and Secondary Schools, by School Type, Canada, Provinces and Territories, 2016/2017," Government of Canada, 2 November 2018, https:// www150.statcan.gc.ca/n1/daily-quotidien/181102/t001c-eng.htm.

80 Deani Van Pelt, *Home Schooling in Canada: The Current Picture – 2015 Edition* (Vancouver: Barbara Mitchell Centre for Improvement in Education, Fraser Institute, 2015), 23, https://www.fraserinstitute.org /research/home-schooling-in-canada-current-picture-2015.

81 Government of Ontario, "Policy/Program Memorandum No. 131," 17 June 2002, http://www.edu.gov.on.ca/extra/eng/ppm/131.html.

82 Ministère de l'Éducation, "Frequently Asked Questions," Gouvernement du Québec, 2020, http://www.education.gouv.qc.ca/en/school-boards /support-and-assistance/homeschooling/frequently-asked-questions/.

83 Canadian Home Based Learning Resource Page, "Home Education Legalities in Quebec," 2020, https://homebasedlearning.ca/provinces /qc/legalities/.

84 Scott Davies and Janice Aurini, "Homeschooling and Canadian Educational Politics: Rights, Pluralism and Pedagogical Individualism,"

Evaluation & Research in Education 17, nos. 2–3 (15 May 2003): 64, https://doi.org/10.1080/09500790308668292.

85 Aurini and Davies, "Choice without Markets," 466, https://doi.org/10.1080/01425690500199834.

86 Cheryl Fields-Smith and Monica Wells Kisura, "Resisting the Status Quo: The Narratives of Black Homeschoolers in Metro-Atlanta and Metro-DC," *Peabody Journal of Education* 88, no. 3 (1 July 2013): 272–6, https://doi.org/10.1080/0161956X.2013.796823. Lisa Puga, "'Homeschooling Is Our Protest:' Educational Liberation for African American Homeschooling Families in Philadelphia, PA," *Peabody Journal of Education* 94, no. 3 (27 May 2019): 283, https://doi.org/10.1080/0161956X.2019.1617579.

87 Kearie Daniel, "Why Black-Canadian Families Are Choosing to Homeschool Their Kids," *Today's Parent*, 26 September 2019, https://www.todaysparent.com/kids/school-age/why-black-canadian-families-are-choosing-to-homeschool-their-kids/.

88 Jennifer L. McCarthy Foubert, "'Damned If You Do, Damned If You Don't:' Black Parents' Racial Realist School Engagement," *Race Ethnicity and Education*, published under latest articles, 20 June 2019: 9–12, https://doi.org/10.1080/13613324.2019.1631782; Aixa D. Marchand et al., "Integrating Race, Racism, and Critical Consciousness in Black Parents' Engagement with Schools," *Journal of Family Theory & Review* 11, no. 3 (2019): 373–5, https://doi.org/10.1111/jftr.12344.

89 Carl E. James, *Colour Matters: Essays on the Experiences, Education, and Pursuits of Black Youth* (Toronto: University of Toronto Press, 2021).

90 Carl E. James, "Who Can/Should Do This Work? The Colour of Critique," in *Revisiting the Great White North?*, ed. D.E Lund and Paul R. Carr (Boston: Sense Publishers, 2015), 141–54.

91 Michael W. Apple, "Away with All Teachers: The Cultural Politics of Home Schooling," *International Studies in Sociology of Education* 10, no. 1 (2000): 75, https://doi.org/10.1080/09620210000200049.

92 Waslander, Pater, and van der Weide, "Markets in Education," 14–16; Rowe and Lubienski, "Shopping for Schools," 352.

93 R. Allison Roda and Amy Stuart Wells, "School Choice Policies and Racial Segregation: Where White Parents' Good Intentions, Anxiety, and Privilege Collide," *American Journal of Education* 119, no. 2 (1 February 2013): 289, https://doi.org/10.1086/668753.

94 James Joseph Scheurich and Linda Skrla, *Leading for Equity and Excellence: Creating High Achievement Classrooms, Schools, and Districts* (Thousand Oaks, CA: Corwin, 2003), 79–98.

95 People for Education, *2019 Annual Report on Schools: What Makes a School?* (Toronto: People for Education, 2019), https://peopleforeducation .ca/report/2019-annual-report-on-schools-what-makes-a-school/.

96 "'It Was a Joke': Students Describe Lax Standards, Easy High Marks at Private Schools Known as 'Credit Mills,'" CBC Radio, The Doc Project, 28 January 2020, https://www.cbc.ca/radio/docproject/it-was-a-joke -students-describe-lax-standards-easy-high-marks-at-private-schools -known-as-credit-mills-1.5436192.

97 Tammie Sutherland, "GTA Secondary Schools Faking Grades in Exchange for Cash," CityNews Toronto, 29 July 2019, https://toronto .citynews.ca/2019/07/29/gta-secondary-schools-faking-grades-in -exchange-for-cash/.

98 Janice Aurini and Scott Davies, "The Transformation of Private Tutoring: Education in a Franchise Form," *The Canadian Journal of Sociology / Cahiers canadiens de sociologie* 29, no. 3 (2004): 425, https://doi .org/10.2307/3654674.

99 Oxford Learning, "About Us," 2020, https://www.oxfordlearning.com /about-us/.

100 Kumon North America, "Get the Answers to All Your Questions," 2020, https://www.kumon.com/pa-en/frequently-asked-questions.

101 Carmen Chai, "Private Tutoring Is Thriving in Canada, but Is It Necessary?" Global News, 23 October 2013, https://globalnews.ca /news/920126/private-tutoring-is-thriving-in-canada-but-is-it-necessary/.

102 The Math Guru, "Welcome to the Math Guru!" The Math Guru, n.d., https://www.themathguru.ca.

5. Taking Action

1 Caroline Alphonso, "'Pull Back These Cuts': Ontario Teachers Send Unified Message with Mass Rally," *Globe and Mail*, 21 February 2020, https://www.theglobeandmail.com/canada/article-pull-back-these -cuts-ontario-teachers-send-unified-message-with/.

2 CBC News, "'We're All in It for the Kids': Ontario Education Unions Lead Thousands in Job Action," CBC, 21 February 2020, https://www.cbc.ca /news/canada/toronto/ontario-teachers-provincewide-strike-1.5470980.

3 Alphonso, "Pull Back These Cuts."

4 Cillian O'Brien, "Provincewide Strike Sees Two Million Ont. Schoolchildren out of Class," CTV News, 21 February 2020, https://www .ctvnews.ca/canada/provincewide-strike-sees-two-million-ont -schoolchildren-out-of-class-1.4822131.

5 Isabel Teotonio, "Does Money Matter? A Look at One of the Key Issues in Ontario Teachers' Battle with the Province," *Toronto Star*, 21 February 2020, https://www.thestar.com/news/gta/2020/02/21/does-money-matter-a-look-at-one-of-the-key-issues-in-ontario-teachers-battle-with-the-province.html.

6 CBC News, "'We're All in It for the Kids.'"

7 Joe L. Kincheloe, "Critical Democracy and Education," in *Understanding Democratic Curriculum Leadership*, ed. James G. Henderson and Kathleen R. Kesson (New York: Teachers College Press, 1999), 73.

8 Michael W. Apple, *The Struggle for Democracy in Education: Lessons from Social Realities* (New York: Routledge, 2018); John P. Portelli and Christina Patricia Konecny, "Neoliberalism, Subversion and Democracy in Education," *Encounters in Theory and History of Education* 14 (6 November 2013): 90, https://doi.org/10.24908/eoe-ese-rse.v14i0.5044.

9 Support Our Students Alberta, "Our Philosophy," Support Our Students Alberta, 2020, https://www.supportourstudents.ca/.

10 Support Our Students Alberta, "An Open Letter to the Minister of Education," Support Our Students Alberta, 2020, https://www.supportourstudents.ca/.

11 Bernie Froese-Germain et al., *Commercialism in Canadian Schools: Who's Calling the Shots?* (Ottawa: Canadian Centre for Policy Alternatives, 2006).

12 Simon Enoch and Emily Eaton, *Crude Lessons* (Regina, SK: Canadian Centre for Policy Alternatives, 2019), 2, https://www.policyalternatives.ca/publications/reports/crude-lessons.

13 Bernie Froese-Germain, *Public Education: A Public Good* (Ottawa: Canadian Teachers' Federation, 2016).

14 Froese-Germain, *Public Education*, 4.

15 Froese-Germain, 28.

16 Ben Williamson, Rebecca Eynon, and John Potter, "Pandemic Politics, Pedagogies and Practices: Digital Technologies and Distance Education during the Coronavirus Emergency," *Learning, Media and Technology* 45, no. 2 (2 April 2020): 108, https://doi.org/10.1080/17439884.2020.1761641.

17 Google, "Teach from Anywhere," n.d., https://teachfromanywhere.google/intl/en/.

18 Lisa Railton, "Gaggle for Microsoft Teams," 16 April 2020, https://blog.gaggle.net/gaggle-safety-management-for-microsoft-teams.

19 T.J. McCue, "E Learning Climbing to $325 Billion by 2025 UF Canvas Absorb Schoology Moodle," *Forbes*, accessed 28 May 2020, https://www.forbes.com/sites/tjmccue/2018/07/31/e-learning-climbing-to-325-billion-by-2025-uf-canvas-absorb-schoology-moodle/.

20 Wendy Brown, "American Nightmare: Neoliberalism, Neoconserv-
    atism, and De-Democratization," *Political Theory* 34, no. 6 (2006): 694.
21 John W. Kingdon, "How Do Issues Get on Public Policy Agendas?" in
    Sociology and the Public Agenda, ed. William Julius Wilson (Newbury
    Park, CA: SAGE Publications, 1993), 41.
22 Richard Brennan, "Minister Plotted 'to Invent a Crisis': Snobelen Video
    Spurs Angry Calls for Him to Resign," *Toronto Star*, 13 September 1995,
    final edition, A3.
23 Antoni Verger, Clara Fontdevila, and Adrián Zancajo, "Multiple Paths
    towards Education Privatization in a Globalizing World: A Cultural Po-
    litical Economy Review," *Journal of Education Policy* 32, no. 6 (2 Novem-
    ber 2017): 773, https://doi.org/10.1080/02680939.2017.1318453.
24 Samantha Hedges et al., "Private Actors and Public Goods: A Compara-
    tive Case Study of Funding and Public Governance in K–12 Education in
    3 Global Cities," *Journal of Educational Administration and History* 52, no. 1
    (2 January 2020): 107, https://doi.org/10.1080/00220620.2019.1685474.
25 Verger, Fontdevila, and Zancajo, "Multiple Paths," 773–4.
26 Frank Adamson, Channa Cook-Harvey, and Linda Darling-Hammond,
    *Whose Choice? Student Experiences and Outcomes in the New Orleans School
    Marketplace* (Stanford, CA: Stanford Centre for Opportunity Policy in
    Education, 2015), 6, https://edpolicy.stanford.edu/library
    /publications/1374.
27 Adamson, Cook-Harvey, and Darling-Hammond, *Whose Choice?*, 42.
28 Cassandra Szklarski, "Parents Unhappy with Back-to-School Protocols
    Scramble to Make Alternative Plans," CP24, 3 August 2020, https://
    www.cp24.com/news/parents-unhappy-with-back-to-school-protocols
    -scramble-to-make-alternative-plans-1.5049691.
29 Diane Ravitch, *Slaying Goliath: The Passionate Resistance to Privatization
    and the Fight to Save America's Public Schools* (New York: Alfred A. Knopf,
    2020), 77–81.
30 Nancy Fraser, "Reframing Justice in a Globalizing World," *New Left Re-
    view*, II, no. 36 (2005): 73–4.
31 Richard Wilkinson and Kate Pickett, *The Spirit Level: Why Greater Equal-
    ity Makes Societies Stronger* (New York: Bloomsbury USA, 2011).

Appendix: Steps in Conducting Critical Policy Research

 1 Sue Winton, "The Normalization of School Fundraising in Ontario:
    An Argumentative Discourse Analysis," *Canadian Journal of Educational
    Administration and Policy* 180 (2016): 202–33.

2 Sue Winton, "Coordinating Policy Layers of School Fundraising in Toronto, Ontario, Canada: An Institutional Ethnography," *Educational Policy* 33, no. 1 (1 January 2019): 44–66, https://doi.org /10.1177/0895904818807331.

3 Sue Winton and Michelle Milani, "Policy Advocacy, Inequity, and School Fees and Fundraising in Ontario, Canada," *Education Policy Analysis Archives* 25, no. 40 (24 April 2017): 1–33, https://doi.org/10.14507 /epaa.25.2679.

4 Ontario Ministry of Education, *Fundraising Guideline* (Toronto, ON: Government of Ontario, 2012), http://www.edu.gov.on.ca/eng /parents/fundraising.html, 1.

5 Fazal Rizvi and Bob Lingard, *Globalizing Education Policy* (New York: Routledge, 2010), 54–6; Lesley Vidovich, "Removing Policy from Its Pedestal: Some Theoretical Framings and Practical Possibilities," *Educational Review* 59, no. 3 (2007): 297–8.

6 Sue Winton, *Character Matters! Policy and Persuasion* (Toronto: Ontario Institute for Studies in Education, University of Toronto, 2007).

7 Naomi Nichols and Alison I. Griffith, "Talk, Texts, and Educational Action: An Institutional Ethnography of Policy in Practice," *Cambridge Journal of Education* 39, no. 2 (1 June 2009): 242, https://doi.org /10.1080/03057640902902286.

8 Lois André-Bechely, "Public School Choice at the Intersection of Voluntary Integration and Not-So-Good Neighborhood Schools: Lessons from Parents' Experiences," *Educational Administration Quarterly* 41, no. 2 (1 April 2005): 268–9, https://doi.org/10.1177/0013161X04269593.

9 André-Bechely, "Public School Choice," 269.

10 Maarten A. Hajer, *The Politics of Environmental Discourse: Ecological Modernization and the Policy Process* (Oxford: Clarendon Press, 1997).

11 For example, see Veronica Pacini-Ketchabaow, Jan White, and Ana-Elisa Armstrong de Almeida, "Racialization in Early Childhood: A Critical Analysis of Discourses in Policies," *International Journal of Educational Policy, Research and Practice: Reconceptualizing Childhood Studies* 7, no. 95 (2006): 95–113; Sue Winton and Stephanie Tuters, "Constructing Bullying in Ontario, Canada: A Critical Policy Analysis," *Educational Studies* 41, nos. 1–2 (15 March 2015): 122–42, https://doi.org/10.1080/03055698.2014.955737.

12 For example, see Jill Koyama, "Principals as Bricoleurs: Making Sense and Making Do in an Era of Accountability," *Educational Administration Quarterly* 50, no. 2 (1 April 2014): 279–304, https://doi.org/10.1177 /0013161X13492796; Jill Koyama, "Principals, Power, and Policy:

Enacting 'Supplemental Educational Services,'" *Anthropology and Education Quarterly* 42, no. 1 (2011): 20–36.

13 For example, see Katherine Cumings Mansfield, Anjalé D. Welton, and Margaret Grogan, "'Truth or Consequences': A Feminist Critical Policy Analysis of the STEM Crisis," *International Journal of Qualitative Studies in Education* 27, no. 9 (21 October 2014): 1155–82, https://doi.org/10.1080 /09518398.2014.916006.

14 For example, see Laura Pinto, *Curriculum Reform in Ontario: "Common Sense" Policy Processes and Democratic Possibilities,* (Toronto, ON: University of Toronto Press, 2012); Sue Winton and Michelle Milani, "Policy Advocacy, Inequity, and School Fees and Fundraising in Ontario, Canada," *Education Policy Analysis Archives* 25, no. 40 (24 April 2017): 1–33, https://doi.org/10.14507/epaa.25.2679.

15 For example, see Catherine A. Lugg and Jason P. Murphy, "Thinking Whimsically: Queering the Study of Educational Policy-Making and Politics," *International Journal of Qualitative Studies in Education* 27, no. 9 (2014): 1183–204, https://doi.org/10.1080/09518398.2014.916009.

16 Kathryn E. King, "Method and Methodology in Feminist Research: What Is the Difference?" *Journal of Advanced Nursing* 20, no. 1 (1994): 19–20, https://doi.org/10.1046/j.1365-2648.1994.20010019.x.

17 Sarah Diem and Michelle D. Young, "Considering Critical Turns in Research on Educational Leadership and Policy," *International Journal of Educational Management* 29, no. 7 (20 August 2015): 844, https://doi .org/10.1108/IJEM-05-2015-0060.

18 Michelle D. Young and Sarah Diem, "Introduction: Critical Approaches to Education Policy Analysis," in *Critical Approaches to Education Policy Analysis: Moving Beyond Tradition*, ed. Michelle D. Young and Sarah Diem (Cham, Switzerland: Springer, 2016), 5, http://ebookcentral .proquest.com/lib/york/detail.action?docID=4745441.

19 Erin Atwood and Gerardo R. López, "Let's Be Critically Honest: Towards a Messier Counterstory in Critical Race Theory," *International Journal of Qualitative Studies in Education* 27, no. 9 (21 October 2014): 1139, https://doi.org/10.1080/09518398.2014.916011.

20 Leslie Bartlett and Frances Vavrus, *Rethinking Case Study Research: A Comparative Approach* (New York: Routledge, 2016), 1–6.

Index

Note: Page numbers in italics indicate a table.

access: concept of, 20–1; e-learning, 92; Internet, 94; private schools, 101–2

action, against privatization: challenges 125–9; critical questioning, 122–4; dialogue, public, 125; East End Parents 4 Public Education anecdote, 115–16; free events, 124; information sources, 118–22. *See also* educational privatization; private benefits; school choice policies

Advanced Placement programs (AP), 85, *86*

Agenda with Steve Paikin, The, 118

Allison, Derek, on reasons parents choose private schools, 8

alternative and specialized schools and programs: anecdote about getting into, 74–6; class, 86, 87–8; data on, 87; distinctions, 83–4; as exclusionary, 88, 108; fees for, 61–2; government awareness of inequity, 87; magnet programs, 84; mini schools, 84–5; overview, 83; and public school ideal, 87; race, 83–4, 85–6, *86*, 87–8; student achievement, 84; variety of, 85–6. *See also* educational markets; private benefits; private schooling; school choice policies

Andre-Becheley, Lois, on race and school choice policy, 140

Anglophone South School District, and e-learning, 94

Apple, Michael, on "us" *vs.* "them" mentality, 19

argumentative discourse theory, 140, 143

Association of Franco-Ontarian Teachers, 116

Atlantic Institute for Market Studies (AIMS), 78, 122

Aurini, Janice: on homeschooling, 104, 105; on school choice, 78–9; on tutoring services, 111–12

Avalon East School District, 61

Axelrod, Paul, on historical goals of public education, 25, 26

Backpack Full of Cash (documentary), 120

Ball, Stephen: on endogenous and exogenous privatization, 9; on parenting and class, 58; on policy cycle, 41–2, 135, 138; on policy enactment, 40

Bansel, Peter, on neoliberalism, 57–8

Barman, Jean, on private school funding, 99

Bischof, Harvey, on politics and education, 116

Bosetti, Lynn: on charter schools, 97; on reasons parents choose private schools, 8; and school choice policy, 95

Bowe, Richard, on policy cycle, 41–2, 135, 138

Braun, Annette, on policy enactment, 40

Brent, Brian, on fundraising, 58

British Columbia Teachers' Federation (BCTF), 63–4, 98

Brown, Wendy: on market principles, 126; on neoliberalism, 18

Butterfield, Phil, on charter schools, 97

Canadian Bureau for International Education, 68

Canadian Centre for Policy Alternatives (CCPA), 46, 120–1

Canadian Home Based Learning, 105

Canadian Journal of Educational Administration and Policy, 118

Canadian Parents for French, 89

Canadian Teachers' Federation (CTF), 46, 120, 121

Captive Audience: How Corporations Invaded Our Schools (Gidney), 15, 16

Carlson, Deven, on interdistrict enrolment, 81

casinos, as fundraisers, 47–8

Catholic Archdiocese of Edmonton, 48

C.D. Howe Institute, 78

character education, 134

Charter School Handbook (Alberta), 96

charter schools, 10, 23, 95–7

Charter Schools Regulation (Alberta), 10, 23

Children First: School Choice Trust, 103–4

class: alternative schools, 86, 87–8; e-learning, 92–3, 95; fee waivers, 63–5; French Immersion, 90–1; fundraising advantage, 52; fundraising effects, 57–8; homeschooling, 107; policy, 26, 42; school choice policies, 77, 78–9, 79–80, 81–3, 108, 113–14; specialized programs, 87–8. *See also* race

Classism/Poverty Sub-Committee (York Region District School Board), 65

Commercialism in Canadian Schools: Who's Calling the Shots? (CCPA, CTF, FSE), 120

Contribution of Resources by Parents (New Brunswick), 50, 63

Conversation, The, 118

Cordova-Cobo, Diana, on racially and socioeconomically diverse schools, 82

COVID-19 pandemic: "complementary" *vs.* necessary items, 50–1; e-learning, 94–5, 125–6; learning pods, 77; privatization, 128–9; and schools' custodial function, 24; tutoring services, 112

Crawford, Cameron, on French Immersion program location, 91

Critical Approaches to Education Policy Analysis: Moving Beyond Tradition (Young, Diem), 141

critical democracy, 27–8, 117, 140

critical policy research: anecdote about, 131–3; context, 37–9, 42, 135–8; critical questioning, 122–4; data collection, 141–2, 145; definitions of policy, 40–1, 135; language, 39–40, 41; multiple theory engagement, 139–40; overview, 37, 133; policy appropriation, 40; policy enactment, 40; purpose of, 145; research plan execution, 144–5; research-question development, 138–9; study design, 140–4; topic identification, 133–5. *See also* policy; policy analysis

critical questioning, as strategy, 122–4

critical race theory (CRT), 140, 141

C.S. Mott Children's Hospital National Poll on Children's Health, 61, 63–4

Currin, Elizabeth, and Opt Out Florida study, 37

Daniels, Lyn, on Indigenous students and specialized programs, 87

Davidson-Harden, Adam, on education privatization in Canada, 13–14

Davies, Bronwyn, on neoliberalism, 57–8

Davies, Scott: on homeschooling, 104, 105; on school choice,

78–9; on tutoring services, 111–12

democracy, critical. *See* critical democracy

Deschambault, Ryan, on English language learners, 71–2

Di Bona, Joseph, on fundraising, 58

Diem, Sarah, on policy analysis, 141

discourse, as policy, 41, 135, 141

distributed learning. *See* e-learning

Dockterman, Daniel, on magnet schools and student achievement, 84

East End Parents 4 Public Education, 115–16

educational markets: about, 10–11, 116; alternative and specialized schools and programs, 83–8; alternative school anecdote, 74–6; French Immersion, 10, 85, 88–91; government's role, 67; quasi-markets, 14; roles within, 18–19; school choice policies, 77–80. *See also* free market; international students; private benefits; school choice policies

educational privatization: about, 4–5, 116–17; as active process, 12; and catastrophes, 127–8; contexts, 15–20; criticism of, 20, 24–5; definitions and variations, 4, 8–12, 116; educational markets, 10–11; endogenous, 10, 11, 42, 77; exogenous, 9–10, 11, 15; and government policy, 115–17; individual *vs.* collective good, 11; outside Canada, 20; paths to, 12–15; perpetuates inequality, 27; and private schools, 98–9;

educational privatization (*continued*)
recent developments, 6–8; scaling
up, 13; typology (Lubienski),
9, 11. *See also* action, against
privatization; alternative
and specialized schools and
programs; government;
neoliberalism; private benefits;
private sector involvement;
school choice policies
Education Policy Analysis Archives, 118
Education Project (CCPA), 120
Education Quality and
Accountability Office (EQAO),
31–3, 35, 36
e-learning, 92–5, 125–6
Elementary Teachers' Federation of
Ontario, 116
elite athlete program, 85, *86*, 87
endogenous privatization, 10–11
English Language Learners (ELLs),
32, 71–2, 81, 90, 91
Enhancing Equity Task Force, 62, 87
enrolment: French Immersion, 89–
90; and funding, 77, 98; open, 80–3
exogenous privatization, 9–10, 11

Fallon, Gerald: on government
and educational markets, 67; on
international student funding, 71;
on "quasi-public schools," 21
Farhadi, Beyhan, on e-learning, 92–3
Fédération des syndicats de
l'enseignement, 46, 120
fees: as barrier to participation, 61,
64; charter schools, 96; extras
/ enhancements *vs.* basics,
66; hidden costs, 62; kinds,
60–2; optional fees anecdote,
43–5; parents as funders, 42,

47; parents' support for, 66;
provincial variations, 59–60,
65–6; questioning, 124; resistance,
65–7; and school choice, 107–8;
specialized programs, 87;
waivers, 63–5, 66, 107, 117. *See
also* access; fundraising
Fesseha, Ellen, on testing, 32
Fine Arts Core Education (FACE), 88
Fontdevila, Clara, on paths to
privatization, 12–13
*Food and Nutrition Policy for Nova
Scotia Public Schools* (Nova
Scotia), 50
For the Love of Learning (Royal
Commission on Learning
Report), 38
Fox, Lauren, on racially and
socioeconomically diverse
schools, 82
Fraser Institute, 78, 103, 121–2
free market, 17, 103, 126
Freidus, Alexandra, on fundraising,
57
French Immersion, 10, 85, 88–91
fundraising: administrators,
58–9; amounts raised, 51–2; and
business, 59; class: 57–8; common
strategies, 47; crowdsourcing,
48–9; extras / enhancements
vs. basics, 54; food as, 47; gap,
52–3; and government, 59, 126–7;
government underfunding, 54;
grants, 48, 53; growing intensity
of, 45–6; international students
as, 10, 12, 13, 67–9; opt-in events,
124; parent engagement, 56–7,
126–7; parents as funders, 42, 47;
policies, 49–51; prevalence of,
46–7; as privatization strategy,

126–7; questioning, 124; race, 57; rationale, 53–4; schools' reliance on, 4; winners and losers, 55–9. *See also* fees; Scholastic book fair

Fundraising Guide (TDSB), 54

Fundraising Guideline (Ontario), 50, 137

Fund Raising in Schools (Yukon), 50

"Gaggle for Microsoft Teams," 125–6

Gaztambide-Fernández, Rueben: on race and specialized programs, 85–6, 88

Gidney, Catherine, on privatization, 15, 16

Globalizing Educational Policy (Lingard, Rizvi), 138

Gold, Anne, on policy cycle, 41–2, 135, 138

Google, and e-learning, 125

government: consultation process, 123; educational markets, 67; facilitates privatization, 10, 115–17; funding of public education, 21; and fundraising, 59, 126–7; homeschooling, 104–5; markets, 17; neoliberalism, 98; private schools, 99–100, 102; and private sector, 17–18; specialized programs, 87; underfunding of schools, 54, 73. *See also* educational privatization

Graham, Cameron, on testing and governability, 41

grants, as fundraising, 48, 53

Griffith, Alison, on institutional ethnography, 139–40

Gulson, Kalervo, on parents and French Immersion, 91

Hajer, Martaan, on argumentative discourse theory, 140, 143

Herman, Joan, on magnet schools and student achievement, 84

Hogan, Anna, on meanings of "public," 20

Holt, John, and unschooling movement, 105

homeschooling: background, 104; class, 107; funding, 105, 106–7; government involvement, 104–5; increasing, 7; race, 106; rationale for, 8, 105–6, 129

Honig, Meredith, on implementation research, 35–6

Hoskins, Kate, on policy enactment, 40

Howard, Philip, on Afrocentric school, 83

How Racially Diverse Schools and Classrooms Can Benefit All Students (Wells, Fox, Cordova-Cobo), 82

Hurricane Katrina, 128

Independent School Act (British Columbia), 99

independent schools. *See* private schooling

Indigenous students and families, 26, 42, 77, 79–80, 87, 88, 106, 180

individualized education plans (IEPs), 32, 36

institutional ethnography, 139–40, 141

International Baccalaureate (IB), 10, 46, 83, 85

international students: benefits and costs, 68, 69–73; Canada as destination, 68–9, 72–3, 78; effect on staff, 72, 73; as fundraising, 10, 12, 13; parents as funders,

international students (*continued*)
42; recruitment, 67–9, 71, 72, 117;
urban *vs.* rural districts, 71
In the Ruins of Neoliberalism (Brown), 18

James, Carl, on Afrocentric school, 83
Jang, Eunice Eunhee, on testing, 32
Jann, Werner, on policy stages, 34–5
*Journal for Critical Education Policy
Studies*, 118

Kearns, Laura-Lee, on EQAO
testing, 32, 37
Killoran, Isobel, on French
Immersion program location, 91
Kumon, 112

Lavery, Lesley, on interdistrict
enrolment, 81
learning opportunity index (LOI),
53
Levin, Ben, on public education
characteristics, 20–1
Levinson, Bradley, on policy
appropriation and "authorized"
policies, 40, 41
Lingard, Bob: on meanings of
"public," 20; on policy question
development, 138
Lord Byng, school fees, 60–2, 63
lotteries, 74, 76, 90, 108
Lubienski, Chris: on consumer
model, 77; on school choice,
79–80, 81, 88; typology of
privatization, 9, 11
Lunden, Stephen, on fundraising, 58

magnet programs, 84
Maguire, Meg, on policy enactment,
40

Majhanovich, Suzanne, on
education privatization in
Canada, 13–14
Marcil, Daisye, class action lawsuit,
65
Massey, Don, 54
Math Guru, 113
McCardle, Todd, and Opt Out
Florida study, 37
meritocracy, 18, 19, 64–5, 126
Metro Parents Network, 54
Microsoft, and e-learning, 125–6
Milani, Michelle, on fees, 64, 137
Mindzak, Michael, on support for
public schools, 6–7
mini schools, 84–5
Mockler, Nicole, on meanings of
"public," 20
Mouvement L'école ensemble, 101

Naidoo, Rajani, on appearance of
equal opportunity, 65
neoconservatism, 19
neoliberalism: COVID-19 pandemic,
118; critics of, 24; free-market
ideology, 16–17, 103, 126; and
fundraising, 57–8; and government
policy, 98; individuals *vs.* governments, 18. *See also* educational
privatization
Neu, Dean, on testing and
governability, 41
Newfoundland and Labrador
Teachers' Association, 121
New Orleans Recovery School
District, 128
New Public Management (NPM),
10, 11, 18, 116
Nichols, Naomi, on institutional
ethnography, 139–40

Official Languages Act (Canada), 89
Olssen, Mark, on education policy,
    33, 34
online course. *See* e-learning
Ontario English Catholic Teachers'
    Association, 116
Ontario Families for Public
    Education, 115
Ontario Parent Action Network, 115
Ontario Secondary School Teachers'
    Federation (OSSTF), 116
Ontario Youth Apprenticeship
    Program (OYAP), 85, *86*
Opt Out Florida, 37
Organisation for Economic Co-
    operation and Development, 7
Ottawa-Carleton District School
    Board (OCDSB), and French
    Immersion demand, 90
Our Schools / Our Selves (CCPA), 121
Oxford Learning, 111, 112

Paquette, Jerry, on private school
    funding, 101–2
Parekh, Gillian: on French
    Immersion program location,
    91; on race and specialized
    programs, 85–6, 88
parents: and basis for school choice
    policies, 79; as business salesforce,
    59; class, 57–58; consequences
    of private advantages, 113–14,
    117; as doners, 48; and education
    markets, 18–19; and fee waivers,
    63–5; as funders, 42, 66; as
    fundraisers, 49, 50, 54, 56–7,
    126–7; and homeschooling, 104–5;
    and private school benefits,
    100–1; and private tutoring, 112–13;
    race, 57; support for fees, 66. *See*

also action, against privatization;
    fees
*Passionate Resistance to Privatization
    and the Fight to Save America's
    Public Schools, The* (Ravitch), 129
Peel District School Board, and
    e-learning during COVID-19
    pandemic, 94
People for Education: on fees, 60–1;
    on fee waivers, 65; on fundraising,
    46, 50, 51, 52; on grants, 48; as
    information source, 118–19
Peters, Michael, on education
    policy, 33, 34
Pinto, Laura: on critical democracy,
    27; on standardized testing, 38
policy: class, 42; and educational
    democracy, 4–5, 7; and inequities,
    14–15; and marketization, 16–18;
    neoliberalism / neoconservatism,
    18–19; policy networks, 19–20;
    provincial variation, 59–60; race,
    42. *See also* critical policy research
policy analysis: about, 33–4; critical
    approaches, 37–42; policy cycle,
    34–5, 41–2, 135, 138; traditional
    approaches, 33–7. *See also* critical
    policy research
"policy windows," concept of, 127
Poole, Wendy: on government
    and educational markets, 67; on
    international student funding, 71;
    on "quasi-public" schools, 21
Portelli, John, on critical democracy,
    27
Porter, Ann, on neoconservatism, 19
Posey-Maddox, Linn, on
    fundraising, 56–7
private benefits: alternative school
    anecdote, 74–6; education markets,

private benefits (*continued*)
77–80; outcomes of pursuing,
113–14; overview, 76–7; private
providers of single credits, 110–11;
private tutoring, 111–13, 129;
psychological testing, 109–10, 119;
public funding and privatization
of, 98–9, 101. *See also* alternative
and specialized schools and
programs; educational markets;
school choice policies
private schooling: admissions criteria,
102, 107; background, 97–8; base
funding amounts, 100, *101*; faith-
based, 8, 100; government control,
99–100; increasing, 7–8; inequity
of, 101–2; reasons for, 8; subsidies,
100–1; tax credits, 102; vouchers,
102–4. *See also* alternative and
specialized schools and programs
private sector involvement, 9–10,
11, 14, 15–17, 17–18. *See also*
educational privatization
privatization, educational. *See*
educational privatization
*Privatization of Education: A Political
Economy of Global Education
Reform, The* (Verger, Fontdevila,
Zancajo), 12–13
*Privatization of Schools: Selling
Out the Right to a Quality Public
Education for All* (CCPA), 121
Programme for International
Student Assessment, 7
psychological testing, 109–10, 119
public education: becoming more
private-like, 7; as commodity,
73, 77; defining characteristics,
20–1; differences across Canada,
21–2, *23*; goals of, historical, 25–6;

public consultation, 22–3, 28;
and public interest, 23–4; public
school ideal, 20–5; support for,
6–7; value of, 129–30. *See also*
educational privatization; public
school ideal; public schools
*Public Education a Public Good:
Report on Privatization of K–12
Education in Canada* (CTF), 121
public-private partnerships (PPPs;
P3s), 10, 13–14, 16
public school ideal: as achievable
goal, 109; critical democracy, 27–8;
defined, 20–1, 28; and fees, 66–7;
and government funding, 54–5;
and homeschooling, 106–7; and
international students, 70; need for,
30, 130; private funding in public
education, 73; and private schools,
100, 101–2; public education, 20–5;
and school choice policies, 82–3,
107–8; and single-credit providers,
111; and specialized programs, 87.
See also educational privatization;
public schools
public schools: benefits greater for
some, 26, 59, 73, 116–17; racism
and discrimination, 106, 107; types
of, *23*. *See also* alternative and
specialized schools and programs;
educational markets; fundraising;
private schooling; public
education; school choice policies
Pyryt, Michael, and school choice
policy, 95

quasi-public, concept of, 21

race: alternative schools,
83–4, 85–6, *86*, 87, 88;

critical policy research on, 139–40; fundraising effects, 57; homeschooling, 106; marginalized groups, space for, 76; policy, 26, 42; school choice policies, 77, 78–9, 79–80, 81–3, 108, 113–14; specialized programs, 87–8. *See also* class

Racial Categories across Selected In-school Programs 2011–12, *86*

Rahimi, Mark, on meanings of "public," 20

Ravitch, Diane, on school choice policies, 129

Re-reading Education Policies: A Handbook Studying the Policy Agenda of the 21st Century (Simons, Olssen, Peters), 33

Rezai-Rashti, Goli, on policy context and enactment, 38, 39, 40

Rizvi, Fazal, on policy question development, 138

Robertson, Heather-jane, "privatization by stealth," 10

Sandals, Liz, on international education, 70

Saskatchewan Teachers' Federation, 49

Scholastic book fair, 3–4, 49, 58–9

SchoolCash Online, 43–4

school choice policies: alternative school anecdote, 74–6; assumptions, underlying, 79; charter schools, 95–7; class, 77, 78–9, 81–3, 108, 113–14; e-learning, 92–5; and homeschooling, 104–7; open enrolment, 80–3; and private schools, 97–104; and public

school ideal, 82–3, 107–8; race, 77, 78–80, 81–3, 108, 113–14; segregation and stratification effects, 107–9, 116–17, 130; and transportation, 81–2; vouchers, 102–4. *See also* action, against privatization; educational markets; educational privatization; private benefits

School Improvement Plans, 38

school type: public and quasi-public, 23; specialized and alternative, 83–4. *See also* alternative and specialized schools and programs; public schools

Schroeder, Stephanie, and Opt Out Florida study, 37

Segeren, Allison, on policy context and enactment, 38, 39, 40

Sen, Vicheth, on international student funding, 71

Sherlock, Tracy, on French Immersion demand, 90

Simons, Maarten, on education policy, 33, 34

Snobelen, John, and crisis invention, 127

Solomon, Patrick, on critical democracy, 27

special education needs: e-learning, 93, 94; endogenous privatization, 42; exclusion of those with, 88, 90, 91, 102; funding, 93, 98, 100; inadequate support of, 32, 94, 110; and private resources, 113, 118–19; schools for those with, *101*, 102, 108; testing wait times, 131, 132

Specialist High Skills Major Program (SHSMP), 85, *86*

Stone, Deborah, on traditional policy analysis, 34
Support our Students (SOS) Alberta, 119–20
Sutton, Margaret, on policy appropriation and "authorized" policies, 40, 41
Sylvan Learning, 111
Syndicat des enseignantes et enseignants du programme francophone de la Colombie-Britannique, 121

teachers, contribute own money, 49, 61
"Teach from Anywhere" (Google), 125
tests: admissions, 96; Education Quality and Accountability Office (EQAO), 31–3; and population governability, 41; Programme for International Student Assessment, 7; psychological, 109–10; responses to, 38–9; TDSB's Afrocentric school, 84; teacher autonomy, 11; wait times, 131
Thompson, Greg, on meanings of "public," 20
Toronto Catholic District School Board (TCDSB), 51
Toronto District School Board (TDSB): Afrocentric public school, 83–4; e-learning, 92–3; French Immersion demographics, 90; funding gap, 52–3; fundraised amounts, 52; fundraising amount per student, 51; *Fundraising Guide,* 54; specialized programs, 85–6

Toronto Social Planning, 53
travel, and single credits, 111

United Conservative Party (UCP) (Alberta), 96–7, 104
unschooling movement, 105

Vancouver District School Board, mini schools, 84–5
Van Pelt, Deani, on reasons parents choose private schools, 8
Verger, Antoni: on catastrophes and privatization, 127–8; paths to privatization, 12–13
Vidovich, Lesley, on policy question development, 138
Vigneault, Stéphane, on private school enrolment, 101
Vincent, Carol, on parenting and class, 58
vouchers, 20, 102–4

Wallin, Dawn, on public education characteristics, 20–1
Wang, Jia, on magnet schools and student achievement, 84
Waters, Johanna, on international student funding, 71, 73
Wegrich, Kai, on policy stages, 34–5
Wells, Amy Stuart, on racially and socioeconomically diverse schools, 82
Wickstrom, Hanna, on testing, 32
Winsa, Patty, on fundraising, 51, 52
Winstead, Teresa, on policy appropriation and "authorized" policies, 40, 41
Wynne, Kathleen, on fundraising, 54

Yoon, Ee-Seul: on Indigenous students and specialized programs, 87; on parents and French Immersion, 91; on school choice, 79–80, 81, 88

York Catholic District School Board, 51

York Region District School Board (Classism/Poverty Sub-Committee), 65

Youdell, Deborah, on endogenous and exogenous privatization, 9

Young, Jon, on public education characteristics, 20–1

Young, Michelle D., on policy analysis, 141

Zancajo, Adrián, on paths to privatization, 12–13

⬤in UTP insights

Books in the Series

- Sue Winton, *Unequal Benefits: Privatization and Public Education in Canada*
- David A. Detomasi, *Profits and Power: Navigating the Politics and Geopolitics of Oil*
- Andrew Green, *Picking up the Slack: Law, Institutions, and Canadian Climate Policy*
- Peter MacKinnon, *Canada in Question: Exploring Our Citizenship in the Twenty-First Century*
- Harvey P. Weingarten, *Nothing Less than Great: Reforming Canada's Universities*
- Allan C. Hutchinson, *Democracy and Constitutions: Putting Citizens First*
- Paul Nelson, *Global Development and Human Rights: The Sustainable Development Goals and Beyond*
- Peter H. Russell, *Sovereignty: The Biography of a Claim*
- Alistair Edgar, Rupinder Mangat, and Bessma Momani (eds.), *Strengthening the Canadian Armed Forces through Diversity and Inclusion*
- David B. MacDonald, *The Sleeping Giant Awakens: Genocide, Indian Residential Schools, and the Challenge of Conciliation*
- Paul W. Gooch, *Course Correction: A Map for the Distracted University*
- Paul T. Phillips, *Truth, Morality, and Meaning in History*
- Stanley R. Barrett, *The Lamb and the Tiger: From Peacekeepers to Peacewarriors in Canada*
- Peter MacKinnon, *University Commons Divided: Exploring Debate and Dissent on Campus*
- Raisa B. Deber, *Treating Health Care: How the System Works and How It Could Work Better*
- Jim Freedman, *A Conviction in Question: The First Trial at the International Criminal Court*
- Christina D. Rosan and Hamil Pearsall, *Growing a Sustainable City? The Question of Urban Agriculture*

- John Joe Schlichtman, Jason Patch, and Marc Lamont Hill, *Gentrifier*
- Robert Chernomas and Ian Hudson, *Economics in the Twenty-First Century: A Critical Perspective*
- Stephen M. Saideman, *Adapting in the Dust: Lessons Learned from Canada's War in Afghanistan*
- Michael R. Marrus, *Lessons of the Holocaust*
- Roland Paris and Taylor Owen (eds.), *The World Won't Wait: Why Canada Needs to Rethink Its International Policies*
- Bessma Momani, *Arab Dawn: Arab Youth and the Demographic Dividend They Will Bring*
- William Watson, *The Inequality Trap: Fighting Capitalism Instead of Poverty*
- Phil Ryan, *After the New Atheist Debate*
- Paul Evans, *Engaging China: Myth, Aspiration, and Strategy in Canadian Policy from Trudeau to Harper*

www.ingramcontent.com/pod-product-compliance
Lightning Source LLC
Chambersburg PA
CBHW030246030426
42336CB00009B/271